VEGETABLE IDENTIFIER

VEGETABLE IDENTIFIER

CHRISTINE INGRAM

LORENZ BOOKS

This edition published in 2001 by Lorenz Books

© 1997, 2001 Anness Publishing Limited

Published in the USA by Lorenz Books
Anness Publishing Inc.
27 West 20th Street
New York
NY 10011

Lorenz Books is an imprint of Anness Publishing Inc.

www.lorenzbooks.com

Previously published as *The New Guide to Vegetables* and,
as part of a larger compendium, *The Vegetable Ingredients
Cookbook*

Publisher: Joanna Lorenz
Senior Cookery Editor: Linda Fraser
Project Editor: Rosemary Wilkinson
Designer: Patrick McLeavey
Cover Design: Balley Design Associates

Photography and Styling: With the exception of sources
noted below, all photographic material supplied and styled
by Patrick McLeavey and Tom Odulate: Gene Colman,
p.70 (bottom); Holt Studios International, p.17 (middle);
Robert Estall, p.38 (top); Michelle Garrett, p.89 (top and
middle); David Jordan, p.79 (top and bottom); MC Picture
Library, p.47 (top), p.74 (bottom); S E Marshall & Co Ltd,
p.36 (bottom); Debbie Patterson, p.88 (top left); Tessa
Traeger, p.25 (bottom); p.84 (top right); The Garden
Picture Library, Sunniva Harte, p.66 (bottom), Mayer/
Le Scanff, p.94 (bottom), p.118 (bottom); Unwins Seeds
Ltd, p.57 (bottom), p.98 (bottom)

Printed and bound in China

10 9 8 7 6 5 4 3 2 1

CONTENTS

INTRODUCTION

Plants have formed an essential part of our diet since the early existence of mankind. Hunter-gatherers progressed towards a more settled life as they learned how to cultivate crops and rear animals. Archaeological evidence indicates that forms of wheat and barley, believed to be the first crops, were farmed in the Middle East as early as 8000 BC. Many edible plants are native to this area, so we can assume that vegetables were also eaten, not least to relieve a monotonous diet. Beans and peas were among the first vegetables farmed in Thessaly and Macedonia.

These legumes would have been enormously important to early societies as they grew easily to provide seeds which were a starchy food, high in protein and which dried well for long storage.

Many of our familiar vegetables were cultivated in historic times: the Egyptians grew onions, garlic, radishes, lettuce and broad beans; the Greeks and Romans farmed produce which was native to their own countries and they also discovered a wider range of plants thanks to their contact with other cultures. By the Middle Ages, a wealth of vegetables was available and recipes for them were recorded in the first cookery books.

NUTRITION

The total contribution of carbohydrate (starchy) foods and vegetables in a well-balanced diet may not be entirely understood, but the benefits and protective role they play in ensuring good health is widely recognized. Expert opinions agree on the fact that we should eat a high proportion of vegetables in our everyday diets.

Although the nutritional value of vegetables varies according to type, freshness, preparation and cooking method, they are a main source of many vitamins, especially vitamin C. Some of the B-group vitamins are also found in vegetables, particularly in green vegetables and pulses. Carrots and dark green vegetables also include carotene which is used by the body to manufacture vitamin A. Vegetable oils are a useful source of vitamin E.

Vegetables also contain calcium, iron, potassium and magnesium, as well as some trace elements which are required in small quantities.

Starchy vegetables are an important source of energy-giving carbohydrate and they may include useful quantities of fibre.

In a vegetarian diet, vegetables, particularly beans, pulses and sprouting seeds, also make a valuable contribution to the overall protein intake.

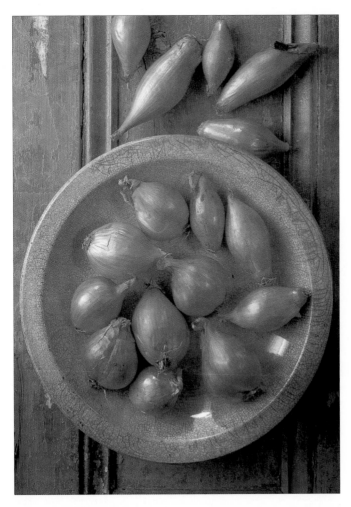

Left: Shallots.

Where specific vegetables within the book are a rich source of nutrients, details are given under the relevant heading.

Vegetables have the highest nutritional content when they are freshly picked. The vitamin content diminishes with staleness and exposure to sunlight. The peel and the layer directly beneath it contain a high concentration of nutrients, so it is best to avoid peeling vegetables or to remove the thinnest layer for maximum nutrient retention.

Minerals and vitamins C and B are water soluble and they are lost by seepage into cooking water or the liquid over which vegetables are steamed. To minimize loss of nutrients, do not cut up vegetables finely as this creates a greater surface area for seepage. Vitamin C is also destroyed by long cooking and by exposure to alkalines.

Raw and lightly cooked vegetables provide the best nutritional value and source of fibre. Any cooking

liquid should, whenever possible, be used in stocks, gravies or sauces.

ABOUT THIS BOOK

There is now available in stores a marvellous range of local and imported vegetables and often a good choice of varieties within each type. This book provides an identification guide to the vegetables of the world, together with essential information on varieties, including what to look for when buying, and how to store, prepare and cook them, so that you can explore the multi-national produce with knowledge and confidence, then make the most of these delicious and nutritious foods in your kitchen.

Above : Curly endive.
Left: Red, orange and green peppers.

ONIONS
AND
LEEKS

Onions

Shallots

Chives

Garlic

Leeks

ONIONS

There are bound to be vegetables you like better than others but a cook would be lost without onions. There are many classic recipes specifically for onion dishes so they can be appreciated in their own right. Onion tarts or French onion soup, for instance, have a sublime flavor, and only onions are appropriate. But also, there is hardly a recipe where onions, or their cousins – garlic, leeks or shallots – are not used. Gently fried until soft, or fried more fiercely until golden brown, they add a unique, savory flavor to dishes.

History

Onions, along with shallots, leeks, chives and garlic, belong to the *Allium* family which, including wild varieties, has some 325 members. All have the characteristic onion smell which is caused by volatile acids beneath the skin.

Archaeological and historical records show that onions have been eaten for thousands of years. They are believed to have originally come from the Middle East and their easy cultivation suggests that their use spread quickly. There are references to the onion in the Bible and it was widely eaten in Egypt. There was, we are told, an inscription on the Great Pyramid stating that the slaves who built the tomb ate their way through 1,600 talents worth of onions, radishes and garlic – presumably a lot, given that the Great Pyramid was made using more than two million 2¹/₂-ton blocks of stone.

By the Middle Ages, onions were a common vegetable throughout Europe and would have been used in soups, stews and sauces when strong flavoring was preferred.

Varieties

As they keep well in a cool place, most people keep a handy stock of onions, usually a general purpose type that can be sautéed or browned. However, onions come in a variety of different colors and strengths, and for certain recipes particular onions are needed.

Right: Spanish onions.
Far right top: Yellow onions.
Far right below: Red onions.

Spanish Onions: Onions raised in warm areas are milder in taste than onions from cooler regions, and Spanish onions are among the mildest cultivated onions. They are a beautiful pale copper color and are noticeably larger than yellow onions. They have a delicate, sweet flavor which makes them ideal for serving raw in salads, thinly sliced, while their size makes them suitable for stuffing and baking whole.

Yellow Onions: These are the widely available onions you find everywhere and, though called yellow onions, their skins are more golden brown. They are the most pungent of all the onions and are a good, all-purpose variety. The smallest ones, referred to as baby, button or pickling onions, are excellent for pickling but can also be added whole to a casserole or sautéed in butter to make a delicious vegetable accompaniment.

Red Onions: Sometimes called Italian onions, these mild onions have an attractive appearance and are now widely available from most good grocers and supermarkets. Below their ruby red skins the flesh is blushed with red. They have a mild, sweet flavor and are excellent thinly sliced and used raw in salads and *antipasti* dishes.

White Onions: These come in all sorts of interesting shapes and sizes – squat, round and oval, big and small. The very small white onions, with shimmery silver skins, are mild and best added whole to stews or served in a creamy sauce. Larger white onions can be mild or strong – there is no way of telling. Like yellow onions, white onions are extremely versatile whether used raw or cooked. The very small white onions, called Paris Silverskin, are the ones used for dry martinis and for commercial pickling.

Vidalia Onions: These popular American onions are a specialty of and named after a town in Georgia. They are a large, pale yellow onion and are deliciously sweet and juicy. Used in salads, or roasted with meat or with other vegetables, they are superb.

Bermuda Onions: These are similar in size to Spanish onions but are more squat. They have a mild flavor and are good thinly sliced, fried until golden and served with steaks or burgers.

remove the next layer of onion, as it is often dry or damaged. Unless slicing onions for stir-fries, for which it is customary to slice the onion into wedges, always slice the onion through the rings, widthwise. Make whole rings, or for half-rings, cut in half lengthwise through the root before slicing (*below*). For finely chopped onion, slice again lengthwise.

Scallions or Spring Onions: These are also true onions but harvested very young while their shoots are still green and fresh. They have a mild, delicate taste and both the small white bulb and the green tops can be used in salads, omelets and stir-fries, or indeed any dish which requires a mild onion flavor.

Nutrition

As well as tasting good, onions are good for you. They contain vitamins B and C together with calcium, iron and potassium. Like garlic, they also contain cycloallin, an anticoagulant which helps protect against heart disease.

Buying and Storing

It used to be a common sight in Europe to see an onion seller traveling around the streets on a bicycle with strings of onions hanging from every available support, including his own neck.

Strings of onions are hard to come by although, if you do find them in stores, they are a good way of buying and

storing the vegetable.

Onions, more than almost any other vegetable, keep well provided they are stored in a cool, dry place, such as a larder or an outhouse. Do not store them in the fridge as they will go soft, and never keep cut onions in the fridge – or anywhere else – unless you want onion-flavored milk and an onion-scented home. Onions do not keep well once cut and it is worth buying onions in assorted sizes so that you do not end up having bits left over. Unused bits of onion can be added to stocks; otherwise throw them away.

Preparing

Onions contain a substance which is released when they are cut and causes the eyes to water, quite painfully sometimes. There are all sorts of ways which are supposed to prevent this, including cutting onions under running water, holding a piece of bread between your teeth or wearing goggles!

As well as the outer brown leaves,

Cooking

The volatile acids in onions are driven off during cooking, which is why cooked onion is never as strong as raw onion. The method of cooking, even the way of frying an onion, affects its eventual taste. Boiled onion or chopped onion added neat to soups or casseroles has a stronger, more raw taste. Frying or sautéing briefly, or sweating (frying in a little fat with the lid on) until soft and translucent gives a mild flavor. When fried until golden brown, onions develop a distinct flavor, both sweet and savory, that is superb with grilled meats and is essential for French onion soup.

Above far left: Vidalia onions.
Left: White onions.
Above left: Large and small scallions.

SHALLOTS

Shallots are not baby onions but a separate member of the onion family. They have a delicate flavor, less intense than most onions and they also dissolve easily into liquids, which is why they are favored for sauces. Shallots grow in small, tight clusters so that when you break one open there may be two or three bunched together at the root.

Their size makes them convenient for a recipe where only a little onion is required. Use shallots when only a small amount of onion is needed or when only a fine onion flavor is required. Shallots are a pleasant, if maybe extravagant, alternative to onions, but where recipes specify shallots (especially sauce recipes), they should be used if possible.

Although classic cooking frequently calls for particular ingredients, the art of improvisation should not be ignored. For instance, Coq au Vin is traditionally made with walnut-size white onions, but when substituted with shallots, the result is delightful.

History

Shallots are probably as ancient as onions. Roman commentators wrote eloquently about the excellence of shallots in sauces.

Varieties

Shallots are small slender onions with long necks and golden, copper-colored skins. There are a number of varieties, although there is unlikely to be a choice in the supermarkets. In any case, differences are more in size and color of skin than in flavor.

Buying and Storing

Like onions, shallots should be firm without any green shoots. They will keep well for several months in a cool dry place.

Preparing and Cooking

Skin shallots in the same way as onions, i.e. top and tail them and then peel off the outer skin. Pull apart the bulbs. Slice them carefully and thinly using a sharp knife – shallots are so small, it is easy to slip and cut yourself. When cooking them whole, fry over very low heat without browning too much.

CHIVES

Chives: In culinary terms, chives are really classed as a herb, but as members of the onion family they are worth mentioning here. As anyone who has grown them knows, chives are tufts of aromatic grass with pretty pale lilac flowers, which are also edible.

Preparing and Serving

Chives are often snipped with scissors and added to egg dishes, or used as a garnish for salads and soups, adding a pleasant but faint onion flavor. Along with parsley, tarragon and chervil, they are an essential ingredient of *fines herbes*.

Chives are also a delicious addition to soft cheeses – far nicer than commercially bought cheeses, where the flavor of chives virtually disappears. Stir also into soft butter for an alternative to garlic butter. This can then be spread onto bread and baked like garlic bread.

If adding to cooked dishes, cook only very briefly, otherwise their flavor will be lost.

Garlic Chives: Garlic chives, sometimes called Chinese chives, have a delicate garlic flavor, and if you see them for sale in your local Chinese supermarket, they are worth buying as they add a delicate onion flavor to stir-fries and other oriental dishes.

Preparing and Serving

Use them as you would chives – both the green and white parts are edible. They are also delicious served on their own as a vegetable accompaniment.

Buying and Storing

For both types of chives, look for plump, uniformly green specimens with no brown spots or signs of wilting. They can be stored for up to a week in the fridge. Unopened flowers on garlic chives are an indication that the plant is young and therefore more tender than one with fully opened flowers.

Above left: Chives.
Above right: Garlic chives.

GARLIC

Garlic is an ingredient that almost anyone who does any cooking at all, and absolutely everyone who enjoys cooking, would not be without.

History

Garlic is known to have been first grown in around 3200 BC. Inscriptions and models of garlic found in the pyramids of ancient Egypt testify to the fact that garlic was not only an important foodstuff but that it had ceremonial significance as well. The Greeks and Romans likewise believed garlic to have magical qualities. Warriors would eat it for strength before going into battle, gods were appeased with gifts of garlic, and cloves of garlic were fastened round the necks of babies to ward off evil. Hence, vampire mythology has ancient precedents.

The Greeks and Romans also used garlic for its therapeutic qualities. Not only was it thought to be an aphrodisiac but also it was believed to be good for eczema, toothache and snake bites.

Although garlic found its way all over Europe – vats of butter, strongly flavored with garlic, have been found by archaeologists working in Ireland which date back 200-300 years – fundamen-tally, its popularity today derives from our liking for Mediterranean, Indian and Asian food, in which garlic plays a very important part.

Nutrition

As is often the case, what was once dismissed as an old wives' tale is, after thorough scientific inquiry, found to be true. Garlic is a case in point; most authorities accept that it has many therapeutic properties. The most significant of these is that it lowers blood cholesterol, thus helping prevent heart disease. Also, raw garlic contains a powerful antibiotic and there is evidence that it has a beneficial effect against cancer and strokes, and increases the absorption of vitamins. Many garlic enthusiasts take their garlic in tablet form, but true devotees prefer to take it as it comes.

Right: A string of pink-skinned garlic.

Varieties

There are numerous varieties of garlic, from the large "elephant" garlic, to small tight bulbs. Their papery skin can be white, pink or purple. Color makes no difference to taste but the particular attraction of the large purple bulbs is that they make a beautiful display in the kitchen.

As a general rule, the smaller the garlic bulb, the stronger it is likely to be. However, most garlic sold in stores is not classified in either shape or form (unless it is elephant garlic) and in practice you will simply pick up whatever you need, either loose, in bunches or on strings.

Garlic grown in a hot climate is likely to be the most pungent, and fresh new season's garlic has a subtle, mild flavor that is particularly good if it is to be used raw, for example, in salads and for dressings.

Above: Elephant garlic beside normal-size bulbs.

Buying and Storing

Garlic bulbs should be firm and round with clear, papery skins. Avoid any that are beginning to sprout. Garlic bulbs keep well stored in a cool, dry place; if the air is damp they will sprout and if it is too warm the cloves will eventually turn to gray powder.

Preparing and Cooking

First break the garlic bulb into cloves and then remove the papery skin. You can blanch this off with hot water but using a fingernail or knife is just as effective. When a garlic clove is split lengthwise a shoot is revealed in the center, which is occasionally green, and some people remove this whatever the color. Cloves are the little segments which make up the bulb and most recipes call for one or more cloves of garlic. (Don't use a bulb when you just need a clove!)

Crush cloves either with the blade of a knife or use a garlic crusher. Crushed garlic cooks more evenly and distributes its flavor in food better than when it is used sliced or finely chopped (stir-fries are the exception). Prepare garlic according to the strength of flavor required: thinly sliced garlic is milder than chopped, which in turn is milder than crushed garlic and, of course, cooking mutes the pungency.

Garlic Breath

The taste and smell of garlic tends to linger on the breath and can be a problem to get rid of. Chewing parsley is a well-known remedy but is only moderately successful. Chewing the seeds of cardamom pods is also said to work but is rather unpleasant. The best suggestion is to eat garlic with your friends so that nobody notices!

LEEKS

Leeks are very versatile, having their own distinct, subtle flavor. They are excellent in pies and casseroles with other ingredients, braised in cream and served by themselves, or simmered in butter as an accompanying vegetable.

Leeks are also wonderful in soups and broths and have rightly earned the title, "king of the soup onions." Cock-a-leekie from Scotland and *Crème Vichyssoise*, invented by the chef of New York's Ritz-Carlton, are two classic leek soups, but many other soups call for leeks.

History

Leeks, like onions and garlic, have a long history. They were grown widely in ancient Egypt and were also eaten and enjoyed throughout the Greek and Roman period. In England, there is evidence that leeks were enjoyed during the Dark Ages. There is little mention of them during the Middle Ages, and history suggests that between the sixteenth and eighteenth centuries eating leeks was not considered fashionable.

However, while they may not have enjoyed a good reputation among the notoriously fickle aristocracy, the rural communities probably continued to eat leeks. They grow in all sorts of climates and are substantial enough to make a reasonable meal for a poor family. It was probably during this time that they were dubbed "poor man's asparagus" – a name which says more about people's snobbishness about food than it does about leeks.

Many place names in England, such as Leckhampstead and Leighton Buzzard, are derived from the word leek and, of course, the leek has been a national emblem of Wales for hundreds of years.

Varieties

There are many different varieties of leeks but among them there is little difference in flavor. Commercially grown leeks tend to be about 10 inches long and about 3/4 inch in diameter. Leeks nurtured in home gardens can be left to grow to an enormous size, but these may develop a woody center.

the first layer of white; then cut a slit from one end to the other through to the center of the leek *(below)*. Wash under cold running water, pulling the sections apart so that the water rinses out any stubborn pieces of earth. If you slice the leeks – either slice thickly or thinly – place them in a colander and rinse thoroughly under cold water.

Cooking

Leeks can be steamed or boiled and then added to your recipe, or you can fry sliced leeks gently in butter for a minute or so and then cover with a lid to sweat so they cook without browning. Unlike onions, leeks shouldn't be allowed to brown; they become tough and unappetizing. They can be stir-fried, however, with a little garlic and ginger. If they begin to cook too fiercely, splash in a little stock and soy sauce and simmer until tender.

RAMP

Among the many wild onions and leeks, the Canadian ramp is perhaps the best known. Also called the wild leek, it looks a little like a scallion, but has a stronger and more assertive garlic-onion flavor. Choose unblemished, clear white specimens with bright, fresh leaves and keep in a cool place, wrapped in a plastic bag to store.

Prepare and cook as you would scallions, by trimming the root end and then slicing thinly. Use in cooking or in salads but remember the onion flavor is stronger, so use sparingly.

Buying and Storing

Buy leeks which look fresh and healthy. The white part should be firm and unblemished and the leaves green and lively. As leeks do not keep particularly well, it is best to buy them as and when you need them. If you need to store them, trim away the top of the leaves and keep them in the salad drawer of the fridge or in a cool place. After several days they will begin to shrivel.

Preparing

It is important to wash leeks thoroughly before cooking as earth and grit lodges itself between the white sections at the base. To prepare leeks, cut away the flags (leaves) and trim the base. Unless the leek is extremely fresh or home-grown, you will probably have to remove

Left: Leeks.
Above: Ramp.

SHOOTS
AND
STEMS

Asparagus

Artichokes

Celery

Celery Root

Fiddlehead Fern

Oriental Shoots

Fennel

Samphire

ASPARAGUS

Asparagus is definitely a luxury vegetable. Its price, even in season, sets it apart from cabbages and cauliflowers, and it has a taste of luxury too. The spears, especially the thick, green spears, at their best in early summer, have an intense, rich flavor that is impossible to describe but easy to remember. If the gods eat, they will eat asparagus – served simply with a good hollandaise!

History

The ancient Greeks enjoyed wild asparagus, but it was not until the Roman period that we know it was cultivated. Even then asparagus was highly thought of: it is recorded that Julius Caesar liked to eat it with melted butter. There is little mention of asparagus being eaten in England until the seventeenth century. Mrs Beeton has 14 recipes for asparagus and from the prices quoted in her cookbook it is apparent that it was expensive even in Victorian times.

Nutrition

Asparagus provides vitamins A, B2 and C and is also a good source of potassium, iron and calcium. It is a well-known diuretic.

Varieties

There are many varieties of asparagus and many different ways of raising it too. Spanish and some Dutch asparagus is white with ivory tips; it is grown under mounds of soil and cut just as the tips begin to show. The purple variety is mostly grown in France, where the spears are cut once the tips are about 1 1/2 inches above the ground. Consequently, the stalks are white and the tops tinged with green or purple. In contrast, American and English asparagus grows above the ground and the spears are entirely green. Arguments continue over which has the better flavor, most growers expressing a preference for their own asparagus!

Thin, short asparagus are excellent when briefly steamed or stir-fried and added to salads. In Italy, they are served by themselves, scattered with grated Parmesan cheese.

Preparing

Unless the asparagus comes straight from the garden, cut off the bottom of the stalk as it is usually hard and woody. If the bottom parts of the stem also feel hard, pare this away with a potato peeler *(below)*. However, if the asparagus is very fresh, this is not necessary, and thin asparagus rarely needs trimming at all.

Cooking

The problem with cooking asparagus is that the stalks take longer to cook than the tender tips, which need to be only briefly steamed. Ideally, use an asparagus steamer. Place the asparagus spears with the tips upward in the wire basket and then lower into a little boiling salted water in the steamer. Cover and cook until the stems are tender.

Alternately, if you don't have an asparagus steamer, place the bundle upright in a deep saucepan of boiling salted water. (The bundle can be wedged into place with potatoes.) Cover with a dome of foil and cook for 5-10 minutes or until the spears are tender. The cooking time depends largely on the thickness of the spears, but it is important not to overcook; the spears should still have a "bite" to them.

Asparagus can also be roasted in a little olive oil. This cooking method intensifies the flavor and is gratifyingly simple. Serve with just a sprinkling of sea salt – it's quite delicious! If steaming asparagus, serve simply with melted butter, which perfectly complements the luxury of the vegetable.

Buying and Storing

Asparagus has a relatively short growing season, from late spring to early summer. Nowadays, it is available in stores almost all year through, but outside the season it will have been imported. It is still good, but it is expensive and will not have the flavor of home-produced asparagus, since it starts to lose its flavor once it is cut.

When buying asparagus, the tips should be tightly furled and fresh looking, and the stalks fresh and straight. If the stalks are badly scarred or droopy, it indicates that they have been hanging around for too long and it is not worth buying. Asparagus will keep for several days if necessary. Untie the bundles and store in the salad drawer of the fridge.

Left: Asparagus.
Above: White asparagus.

ARTICHOKES

Artichokes have an exquisite flavor and are a very sociable food to eat. They grow in abundance in Brittany, and during July and August farmers can frequently be seen selling them by the roadside. The globes are huge hearty specimens and are extremely fresh, so they make a good buy.

History

It is not known for certain whether artichokes were eaten in antiquity. Although they are mentioned by writers, they could have been referring to the cardoon, which is the uncultivated form of artichoke. Cardoons grew wild in many southern European countries, and, as far as we know, cultivated artichokes first became a popular food in Italy. However, Goethe did not share the Italians' liking for the vegetable and remarks in his book, *Travels Through Italy*, that "the peasants eat thistles," something he didn't care for at all.

Nowadays, artichokes are grown all over southern Europe and in California. People in Italy, France and Spain eat artichokes while the vegetable is still young, before the choke has formed and the entire artichoke is edible. Unfortunately, such young delicacies are not exported, but look out for them if you are in these countries.

Buying and Storing

It is only worth buying artichokes when they are in season, although they are available in supermarkets almost all year through. In winter, however, they are sad looking specimens, small and rather dry, and are really not worth the bother of cooking. At their best, artichokes should be lively looking with a good bloom on their leaves, the inner leaves wrapped tightly round the choke and heart inside. Artichokes will keep for 2-3 days in the salad drawer of the fridge but are best eaten as soon as possible.

Preparing and Cooking

First twist off the stalk which should also remove some of the fibers at the base and then cut the base flat and pull away any small base leaves. If the leaves are very spiky, trim them with a pair of scissors if liked *(above)*, then rinse under running water. Cook in boiling water, acidulated with the juice of half a lemon. Large artichokes need to be simmered for 30-40 minutes until tender. To test if they are done, pull off one of the outer leaves. It should come away easily and the base of the leaf should be tender.

heart. Eat the heart with a knife and fork, dipping it in the garlic butter or vinaigrette.

CARDOONS

This impressively large vegetable is closely related to the globe artichoke and has a superb flavor, a cross between artichokes and asparagus. Cultivated plants frequently grow to 6 feet in height, and once mature, cardoons, like celery, are blanched as they grow. This process involves wrapping the stalks with newspaper and black bags for several weeks, so that when harvested, in late fall, before the frosts, the stalks are a pale green.

The cardoon is a popular vegetable in southern Europe but less commonly available elsewhere. In Spain, for instance, it is much appreciated and often appears on the table, poached and served with chestnuts or walnuts. Only the inner ribs and heart are used.

Artichokes and Drink

Artichokes contain a chemical called cynarin, which in many people (although surprisingly not all) affects the taste buds by enhancing sweet flavors. Among other things, this will spoil the taste of wine. Consequently, don't waste good wine with artichokes but drink ice water instead, which should taste pleasantly sweet.

Eating Artichokes

Artichokes are fun to eat. They have to be eaten with fingers, which does away with any pomp and ceremony, always a handicap for a good dinner party.
Serve one artichoke between two, so that people can share the fun of pulling off the leaves and dipping them into garlic butter or vinaigrette. If you want to serve one each, serve them in succession. The dipping sauces are an essential part of eating artichokes; people can either spoon a little onto their plates or have a little bowl each. After dipping, draw the leaf through your teeth, eating the fleshy part.

When most of the leaves have been eaten, a few thin pointed leaves remain in the center, which can be pulled off altogether. Then pull or cut away the fine prickly choke and discard, leaving the

Far left: Artichokes.
Top: Baby artichokes.
Above: Cardoons.

CELERY

Some people say that the very act of
eating celery has a slimming effect
because chewing it uses up more calories than the vegetable itself contains!
Although it may be insubstantial, celery
nevertheless has a distinct and individ-
ual flavor, sharp and savory, which
makes it an excellent flavoring for soups
and stuffings, as well as good on its own
or in salads. The astringent flavor and
crunchy texture of celery contrasts well
with the other ingredients in salads
such as Waldorf salad or Walnut and
avocado salad.

History

Celery is known to have been commonly
eaten in salads in Italy for hundreds of
years.

Nutrition

Celery is very low in calories but contains
potassium and calcium.

Varieties

Most grocers and supermarkets,
depending on the time of year, sell both
green and white celery. When celery is
allowed to grow naturally, the stalks are
green. However, by banking up earth
against the shoots celery is blanched:
the stalks are protected from sunlight
and remain pale and white.
Consequently, white celery is often
"dirty" – covered loosely in soil – while
green celery will always be clean.
White celery, which is frost hardy, is only
available in winter. It is more tender and
less bitter than green celery and is generally considered superior. Celery is
therefore thought of as a winter
vegetable and is traditionally used at
Christmas time, for stuffing and as a
sauce to go with turkey or ham.

Buying and Storing

White celery is in season during the
winter months. If possible, buy "dirty"
celery which hasn't been washed. It has
a better flavor than the pristine but
rather bland supermarket variety. Look
for celery with green fresh-looking leaves
and straight stems. If the leaves or any
outer stalks are missing, it is likely to be
old, so worth avoiding.

Celery will keep for several days in the salad drawer of the refrigerator. Limp celery can be revived by wrapping it in absorbent paper and standing it in a jar of water.

Preparing

Wash if necessary and pull the stalks apart, trimming the base with a sharp knife. Cut into thick or thin slices according to the recipe. When served raw and whole, the coarse outer "strings" should be removed from each stalk by pulling them up from the base.

Cooking and Serving

Serve celery raw and finely sliced in salads, mixed with cream cheese or sour cream. Braised celery is tasty, either whole or sliced. Celery has a distinctive, savory, astringent flavor so is excellent in soups or stuffings.

CELERY ROOT

Strictly speaking, celery root is classified as a root vegetable rather than a shoot or stem. It is knobbly with a patchy brown/white skin and has a similar but less pronounced flavor than celery. Grated and eaten raw, it has a crunchy texture, but when cooked it is more akin to potatoes. Thin slices of potato and celery root cooked *au gratin* with cream is a popular way of serving this vegetable.

Buying and Preparing

If possible, buy smallish bulbs of celery root. The flesh discolors when exposed to light, so as soon as you have peeled, sliced, diced or grated the celery root, plunge it into a bowl of acidulated water (water with lemon juice added).

Cooking

Celery root can be used in soups and broths, or can be diced and boiled and eaten in potato salads.

Left: Green celery.
Above: White celery.
Right: Celery root.

FIDDLEHEAD FERN

Sometimes called the ostrich fern, these shoots are a rich green color and are normally about 2 inches long. They have an unusual flavor, something like a cross between asparagus and okra, and have a slightly chewy texture, which makes them a popular choice for oriental dishes.

Preparing and Cooking

To prepare and cook, trim the ends and then steam or simmer in a little water or sauté in butter until tender. Use in salads or serve as a first course with a hollandaise sauce.

Right: Fiddlehead ferns.
Below left: Alfalfa sprouts.
Below right: Mung bean sprouts.

ORIENTAL SHOOTS

BAMBOO SHOOTS

In the Far East, edible bamboo shoots are sold fresh in the market. The young shoots are stripped of their brown outer skins and the insides are then eaten. Although fresh bamboo shoots can occasionally be found in oriental stores, the most readily available variety is sold in cans. The flavor is undoubtedly spoiled. Fresh bamboo shoots have a mild but distinct taste, faintly reminiscent of artichokes, while canned ones really taste of nothing at all. However, the texture, which, in Chinese cuisine particularly, is as important as the flavor, is not so impaired, and bamboo shoots have a pleasantly crunchy bite.

Preparing and Cooking

Peel away the outer skin and then cook in boiling water for about half an hour. They should feel firm, but not "rock" hard. Once cooked, slice thinly and serve by themselves as a side dish, with garlic butter or a sauce, or add to stir-fries, spring rolls or any oriental dish

where you need a contrast of textures. Since canned bamboo shoots have been preserved in brine, always rinse well before using.

BEAN SPROUTS

Bean sprouts are a neglected vegetable, used almost carelessly for oriental dishes

but otherwise passed by as being insipid and not very interesting. It's a reputation they don't deserve: not only do they have a lovely fresh flavor, but they are also good for you.

All sorts of seeds can be sprouted, but the bean family are favorites among the sprouted vegetables. The bean sprouts most commonly available in the shops are sprouted mung beans, but aduki beans, alfalfa, lentils and soy beans can all be sprouted and taste delicious.

Nutrition

Bean sprouts contain a significant amount of protein, Vitamin C and many of the B vitamins. They have an excellent flavor too, best appreciated eaten raw in salads or sandwiches, and for slimmers they are an ideal food, low in calories, yet with sufficient substance to be filling, and with a flavor and texture that can be enjoyed without a dressing.

Buying and Storing

Bean sprouts should only be bought when absolutely fresh. They don't keep for long and they will taste sour if past their best. The sprouts should be firm, not limp, and the tips should be green or yellow; avoid any that are beginning to turn brown.

Cooking

If stir-frying, add the bean sprouts at the last minute so they cook for the minimum period to keep plenty of crunch and retain their nutritional value. Most health food shops will have instructions on sprouting your own beans. Only buy seeds intended for sprouting.

PALM HEARTS

Fresh palm hearts are the buds of cabbage palm trees and are considered a delicacy in many parts of the world. They are available canned from oriental stores, but are most prized when fresh. These should be blanched before being cooked to eliminate any bitterness. They can be braised or sautéed and then served hot with a hollandaise sauce, or cold with a simple vinaigrette.

WATER CHESTNUTS

Water chestnut is the common name for a number of aquatic herbs and their nut-like fruit, the best known and most popular variety being the Chinese water chestnut, sometimes known as the Chinese sedge. In China they are grown in exactly the same way as rice, the plants needing the same conditions of

high temperatures, shallow water and good soil. In spring, the corms are planted in paddy fields which are then flooded to a depth of some 4 inches. These are drained in fall, and the corms are harvested and stored over the winter. Water chestnuts are much used in Chinese cooking and have a sweet crunchy flavor with nutty overtones.

They are edible cooked or raw and are excellent in all sorts of Chinese dishes.

Above: Sprouting mung beans.
Below: Clockwise from top left: Canned Water chestnuts, canned Bamboo shoots, fresh Water chestnuts, canned Palm hearts.

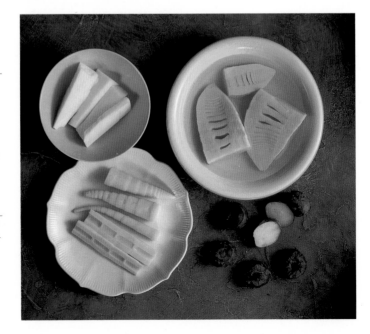

FENNEL

The vegetable fennel is closely related to the herb and spice of the same name. It is called variously bulb fennel, Florence fennel, sweet fennel, *finocchio dulce* or Italian fennel.

Like the herb, Florence fennel has the distinct flavor of anise, a taste that seems to go particularly well with fish, so the vegetable is often served with fish dishes while the herb or spice is commonly used in fish stocks, sauces or soups. The leaves are edible and can be used in soups and stocks as well as for garnishing.

History

Bulb fennel has only been popular for the last ten or so years, although it has a long history of cultivation, having been eaten by the ancient Egyptians, Greeks and Romans. In Italy, fennel has been eaten for several centuries: many of the best fennel recipes come from Italy and other parts of the Mediterranean.

Buying and Storing

If possible, buy small tender bulbs. The bulbs should be clean and white with no bruises or blemishes and the feathery leaves should be green and lively. Fennel will keep for a day or two in the salad drawer of the fridge.

Preparing

Unless the bulbs are very young and tender, remove the first layer of skin, as it is likely to be tough (this can be used for a stock). Fennel can then be sliced into slivers by cutting downward or into rings by cutting across the bulb. When used raw in salads, it must be cut into smaller pieces.

Cooking and Serving

Fennel can be served raw if it is thinly sliced and dressed with a light vinaigrette. In salads, its flavor contrasts well with apple, celery and other crunchy ingredients. Fennel is also excellent braised with onions, tomatoes and garlic.

Right: Bulb fennel.
Far right: Marsh samphire.

SAMPHIRE

There are two types of samphire. Marsh samphire grows in estuaries and salt marshes while rock samphire, sometimes called sea fennel, grows on rocky shores. The two are understandably confused since they are both connected with the sea, yet they are completely different plants.

The type likely to be sold by a fish dealer is marsh samphire. It is also known as glasswort and is sometimes called sea asparagus, as its shoots are similar to small asparagus shoots.

Although marsh samphire grows easily and is commonly found all over North America and Europe, it is not cultivated and is only available for a short time while it is in season, normally in late summer and early autumn.

Samphire has a distinctly salty, iodine flavor and a pleasant crisp texture. The flavor is reminiscent of the sea and goes particularly well with fish and seafood. However, samphire can be enjoyed simply steamed and dipped into melted butter.

Buying and Storing

When in season, good fish dealers get regular stocks of marsh samphire, and it should look bright and fresh. Buy it as you need it, as it will not keep for long.

Preparing and Cooking

If necessary, wash marsh samphire under cold running water. It is best steamed over a pan of boiling water for no more than 3 minutes. Alternately, blanch it in boiling water for 3-5 minutes and then drain. Samphire can be eaten raw but blanching it removes some of the saltiness.

To eat samphire, draw the shoots through the teeth to peel the succulent part from the thin central core.

THREE

ROOTS

POTATOES

History

The potato originates from South America. Most people learned at school that Sir Walter Raleigh brought the tubers to England from Virginia, but this never convinced historians as the potato was completely unknown in North America until the eighteenth century. They now believe that Sir Francis Drake was responsible. In 1586, after battling against the Spaniards in the Caribbean, Drake stopped to pick up provisions from Cartegena in northern Colombia – and these included tobacco and potato tubers. En route home, he stopped off at Roanoke Island, off the coast of Virginia. The first group of English colonists had been sponsored to settle there by Sir Walter Raleigh, but by this time they had had enough. Drake brought them back to England, along with some of Raleigh's men and, of course, the provisions – including the potato tubers.

Potatoes apparently fascinated Queen Elizabeth and intrigued horticulturists, but they were not an overnight success among the people. The wealthy frequently reviled them as being flavorless and the food of the poor. People distrusted the fact that they reached maturity underground, believing them to be the work of

the devil. In Scotland, Presbyterian ministers darkly advised their congregations that there was no mention of potatoes in the Bible, and thus the eating of them was an ungodly act!

In spite of such a bad press, potatoes nevertheless were slowly recognized for their merit. By 1650 they were the staple food of Ireland, and elsewhere in Europe potatoes began to replace wheat as the most important crop, both for people and for livestock. In an early English cookbook, *Adam's Luxury and Eve's Cookery*, there are 20 different recipes for cooking and serving potatoes.

The first mention of potatoes in America is in 1719 in Londonderry, New Hampshire. They arrived not from the south, but via Irish settlers who brought their potatoes with them.

The current popularity of potatoes is probably thanks to a Frenchman called Antoine-Auguste Parmentier. A military pharmacist of the latter part of the eighteenth century, Parmentier recognized the virtues of the potato, both for its versatility and as an important food for the poor, and set out to improve its image. He persuaded Louis XVI to let him ostentatiously grow potatoes on royal land around the palace in Versailles to

impress the fashion-conscious Parisians. He also produced a court dinner in which each course contained potatoes. Gradually, eating potatoes became chic, first among people in the French court and then in French Society. Today, if you see *Parmentier* in a recipe or on a menu, it means "with potato."

Nutrition

Potatoes are an important source of carbohydrate. Once thought to be fattening, we now know that, on the contrary, potatoes can be an excellent part of a calorie-controlled diet – provided, of course, they are not fried in oil or mashed with too much butter. Potatoes are also a very good source of vitamin C, and during the winter potatoes are often the main source of this vitamin. They also contain potassium, iron and vitamin B.

Varieties

There are more than 400 international varieties of potato, but unless you are a gardener, you will find only some 15 varieties generally available. Thanks to labeling laws, packaged potatoes carry their names, which makes it easier to learn to differentiate between the varieties and find out which potato is good for what.

New Potatoes

Carlingford: Available as a new potato or as main crop, Carlingford has a close white flesh.
Jersey Royal: Often the first new potato of the season, Jersey Royals have been shipped from Jersey for over a hundred years and have acquired an enviable reputation among everyone who enjoys good food. Boiled or steamed and then served with butter and a sprinkling of parsley, they cannot be beaten.

Jersey Royals are kidney-shaped, with yellow firm flesh and a distinctive flavor. Don't confuse Jersey Royals with Jersey Whites, which are actually Maris Pipers, grown in Jersey.
Maris Bard: A regularly shaped, slightly waxy potato with white flesh.
Maris Peer: This variety has dry firm flesh and a waxy texture and doesn't disintegrate when cooked – consequently, it is good in salads.

Main Crop Potatoes

Desiree: A potato with a pink skin and yellow soft-textured flesh. It is good for baking, frying, roasting and mashing.

Yukon Gold: A good masher with yellow flesh and pale skin.

Idaho: A russet-skinned potato that was the original favorite for making chips. It has an excellent, distinctive flavor, and should you find them for sale, buy them at once for baked potatoes. They are also good boiled or roasted.

Kerr's Pink: A good cooking potato with pink skin and creamy flesh.

King Edward: Probably the best known of potatoes, although not the best in flavor. King Edwards are creamy white in color with a slightly floury texture.

Red King Edwards are virtually identical except for their red skin. Both are good roasted or baked. However, the flesh disintegrates when boiled, so while good for mashing do not use King Edwards if you want whole boiled potatoes.

Maris Piper: This is a widely grown variety of potato, popular with growers and cooks because it is good for all kinds of cooking methods – baking, frying, roasting and mashing. It has a pale, smooth skin and creamy white flesh.

Left: Maris Bard potatoes.
Above: Kerr's pink (left) and Maris Piper (right) potatoes.
Right: Romano potatoes.

Pentland Dell: A long, oval-shaped potato with a floury texture that tends to disintegrate when boiled. For this reason, it is popular for roasting as the outside becomes soft when parboiled and then crisps up with the fat during roasting.

Romano: The Romano has a distinctive red skin with creamy flesh and is a good all-rounder, similar to Desiree.

Wilja: Introduced from Holland, this is a pale, yellow-fleshed potato with a good, sweet flavor and waxy texture.

Other Varieties

Although most of these varieties are also main crop, they are less widely available than those listed above but are increasingly sold in supermarkets. They are recommended for salads but many are also excellent sautéed or simply boiled.

Cara: A large main crop potato, which is excellent baked or boiled but is a good all-rounder.

Fingerlings: Thumb-sized, long baby potatoes are sometimes called finger potatoes. Among the many varieties are the German Lady's Finger. Since they are new crop potatoes, they need simply be boiled and then served either in salads or with a little butter and a sprinkling of parsley.

La Ratte: A French potato with a smooth skin and waxy yellow flesh. It has a chestnut flavor and is good in salads.

Linzer Delikatess: These small, kidney-shaped potatoes look a little like Jersey Royals but have a pale smooth skin. They do not have much taste and are best in salads where their flavor can be enhanced with other ingredients.

Pink Fir Apple: This is an old English variety, with pink skin and a smooth yellow flesh. It is becoming increasingly popular and has a distinctive flavor.

Above left: Cara (left) and Yukon Gold (right) potatoes.
Left: Linzer Delikatess potatoes.
Above: Desiree (left) and King Edward (right) potatoes.
Right: Fingerlings.

Blue: If you want to startle your friends, serve some of these striking purple-blue potatoes. There are several varieties of blue potato, ranging from a pale lavender to a wonderful deep purple. They have a dense texture, which makes them good for boiling. They are best served simply with a little butter and do retain their color when cooked.

Truffe de Chine: Another deep purple, almost black potato, of unknown origin but now grown in France. It has a nutty, slightly mealy flavor and is best served in a salad with a simple dressing. Like the Blue Potato, it retains its color after being cooked.

Recommended Varieties for Cooking

Baking: As for roasting, use potatoes with a floury texture, such as Idaho, Pentland Dell, King Edward and Maris Piper.

Boiling: Jersey Royal, Maris Bard and Maris Peer, or any of the Egyptian or Belgian new crop varieties. In addition, Pink Fir Apple, La Ratte and Linzer Delikatess are excellent.

Frying: King Edward, Idaho, Romano, Maris Piper and Desiree.

Mashing: Idaho, Maris Piper, King Edward, Wilja, Romano and Pentland Dell and Yukon Gold.

Roasting: Pentland Dell, Idaho, Maris Piper, King Edward, Desiree and Romano are among the best roasting potatoes. Ideally, use potatoes with a floury texture.

Salads: All the small, specialist potatoes, such as La Ratte, Pink Fir Apple and Linzer Delikatess as well as Fingerlings and small new potatoes.

Sautéing: Any waxy type of potato, such as Maris Bard, Maris Peer, any of the specialist potatoes, and Romano and Maris Piper.

Buying and Storing

Potatoes should always be stored in a dark, cool, dry place. If they are stored exposed to the light, green patches will develop which can be poisonous, and they will go moldy if kept in the damp. When buying potatoes in bulk, it is best to buy them in paper sacks rather than plastic bags as humid conditions will cause them to go rotten. Similarly, if you buy potatoes in plastic bags, remove them when you get home and place them in a vegetable rack or in a paper bag, in a dark place.

Main crop potatoes will keep for several months in the right conditions but will gradually lose their nutritional value. New potatoes should be eaten within two or three days as they will go moldy if stored for too long.

Preparing

Most of the minerals and vitamins contained in potatoes are contained in or just below the skin. It is therefore better to eat potatoes in their skins. New potatoes need only be washed under running water; older potatoes need to be scrubbed.

If you peel potatoes, use a peeler that removes only the very top surface (*below left*) or, alternately, for salads and cold dishes, boil the potatoes in their skins and peel when cool.

Cooking

Baking: Cook baked potatoes in a low oven for well-browned and crunchy skins and fluffy flesh. Baked potatoes can be cooked more quickly in a microwave oven; for a crunchy texture to the skin place them in a hot oven for 10 minutes.

Boiling: It is impossible to generalize on how long to boil as it depends so much on the variety of potato. Try to cut potatoes to an even size (new potatoes should not need to be cut), salt the water if liked, cover and cook over a moderate heat. Don't boil potatoes too fiercely; old ones especially may disintegrate and leave you with a pan of starchy water.

French fries: Home-cooked French fries are a treat worth occasionally giving the family instead of the convenient but otherwise disappointing oven fries. However, they are fatty and therefore not good for you when eaten in great quantities or too often.

To make them, cut the potatoes into even-size pieces and place in a bowl of cold water for about 10 minutes before frying. Drain and then dry in a piece of muslin or an old dish towel before frying. Fry only as many pieces as will comfortably sit in the fat. Halfway through cooking, drain them and allow the oil to come back to temperature before plunging the fries back in. This browns the fries and they don't soak up excessive amounts of oil. Be warned; the cooking smells from making fries tend to linger!

Mashing: Boil the potatoes until tender, drain thoroughly and then tip them back into the pan; mash with a little milk and butter using a potato masher (*below right*), and season to taste with a little salt, if necessary, and pepper. Never use a food processor or blender: the potatoes will turn into an inedible thick gray paste. You may lightly whisk potatoes with a fork after mashing to fluff them up, but no more – for once modern machines have not improved on the basic utensil.

Roast Potatoes: The best roast potatoes are made using a floury textured potato such as Maris Piper or King Edward. Wash and cut them into even-size chunks and parboil them in lightly salted water until they begin to go tender and the outside looks soft. Drain them through a strainer or colander and then tip them back into the saucepan, put the lid on and shake the pan two or three times. This roughens up the surface of the potato. Place the potatoes in a dish of hot oil or fat, or around a joint of meat, and turn them over so that they are evenly coated. Roast them in the oven for 40-50 minutes until golden. Serve as soon as possible once cooked as the outsides become leathery if they are kept in a warm oven for too long.

Sautéing: There are various ways to sauté potatoes and no one way is better than another. For sautéed sliced potatoes, parboil whole potatoes for 5-10 minutes until they begin to soften. Drain them thoroughly and then slice into thick rounds. Using sunflower oil or a mixture of sunflower and olive oil (not butter as it will burn), fry them in a large frying pan. Turn the potatoes occasionally and cook until evenly browned. For sautéed, diced potatoes, cut the potatoes into small cubes, blanch for 2 minutes and then drain well. Either fry them on the stove or cook them in a little oil in the oven; turn them once or twice to brown evenly.

Steaming: New potatoes are excellent steamed. Place them on a bed of mint in a steamer or a colander over a pan of boiling water for 15-20 minutes.

Above left: Blue potatoes.
Below left: Truffe de Chine (left) and Pink Fir Apple (right) potatoes.

PARSNIPS

There's something very old-fashioned about parsnips. They conjure up images of cold winter evenings and warm comforting broths supped in front of a blazing wood fire. Nowadays parsnips are available all year through, but many people still feel they belong to winter, adding their characteristic flavor to soups and stews.

Parsnips are related to carrots, similarly sweet but with a distinct earthy flavor that blends well with other root vegetables and is also enhanced with spices and garlic.

History

Parsnips have a long history. The Romans grew and cooked them to make broths and stews. When they conquered Gaul and Britain, the Romans discovered that root vegetables grown in northerly areas had a better flavor than those grown in the south – they may have been the first to decree that parsnips should be eaten after the first frost!

Throughout the Dark Ages and early Middle Ages, parsnips were the main starchy vegetable for ordinary people (the potato had yet to be introduced). Parsnips were not only easy to grow but were a welcome food to eat during the lean winter months. They were also valued for their sugar content. Sweet parsnip dishes like jam and desserts became part of traditional English cookery, and they were also commonly used for making beer and wine. Parsnip wine is still one of the most popular of the country wines, with a beautiful golden color and a rich sherry-like flavor.

Nutrition

Parsnips contain moderate amounts of vitamins A and C, along with some of the B vitamins. They are also a source of calcium, iron and potassium.

Buying and Storing

Parsnips are really a winter crop, although nowadays they are available all year through. Tradition has it that parsnips are best after the first frost, but many people like the very young tender parsnips available in the early summer. When buying parsnips, choose small or

medium-size specimens as the large ones tend to be rather fibrous. They should feel firm and be a pale ivory color without any sprouting roots. Store parsnips in a cool place, ideally an airy larder or cool outhouse, where they will keep well for 8-10 days.

Preparing

Very small parsnips need little or no peeling; just trim the ends and cook according to your recipe. Medium-size and large parsnips must be peeled. Larger parsnips also must have the woody core removed; if it is cut out before cooking, the parsnips will cook more quickly and evenly.

Cooking

Roast parsnips are best parboiled for a few minutes before adding to the roasting dish. Very young parsnips can be roasted whole but larger ones are best halved or quartered lengthwise. Roast in butter or oil for about 40 minutes in an oven preheated to 400°F .

To boil parsnips, cut them into pieces about 2 inches long and boil for 15-20 minutes until tender. When boiled briefly like this, they keep their shape, but when added to a casserole or stew they eventually disintegrate. Don't worry if this happens; parsnips need plenty of cooking so that the flavor can blend with the other ingredients.

JERUSALEM ARTICHOKES

Jerusalem artichokes are related to the sunflower and have nothing to do with Jerusalem. One explanation for their name is that they were christened girasole, "Jerusalem," because their yellow flowers turned toward the sun. The Italian name for the Jerusalem artichoke is *girasole articocco*.

These small knobbly tubers have a lovely distinct flavor and are good in Palestine soup, a popular classic recipe. They are also delicious baked or braised.

History

Jerusalem artichokes are thought to have come from the central United States and Canada, where they were cultivated by the Native Americans as long ago as the fifteenth century. However, many writers have alluded to the fact that they cause "wind," which tempers their popularity.

Buying and Storing

Jerusalem artichokes are at their best during winter and early spring. They are invariably knobbly, but if possible buy neat ones with the minimum of knobs to save waste. The skins should be pale brown without any dark or soft patches. If they are stored in a cool dark place they will keep well for up to 10 days.

Preparing

The white flesh of artichokes turns purplish brown when exposed to light, so when peeling or slicing them raw, place them in a bowl of acidulated water (water to which the juice of about half a lemon has been added). Because artichokes are so knobbly, it is often easier to boil them in acidulated water in their skins and peel them afterward – the cooked skins should slip off easily.

Cooking

Jerusalem artichokes can be cooked in many of the ways in which you would cook potatoes or parsnips. They are excellent roasted, sautéed or dipped in batter and fried, but first parboil them for 10-15 minutes until nearly tender. For creamed artichokes, mix with potatoes in equal amounts; this slightly blunts their flavor, making a tasty side dish which is not too overpowering.

Left: Parsnips.
Below: Jerusalem artichokes.

TURNIPS AND RUTABAGAS

Turnips and rutabagas are both members of the cabbage family and are closely related to each other – so close that it is not surprising that their names are often confused. For instance, rutabagas are sometimes called Swedish turnips or swede-turnips and in Scotland, where they are thought of as turnips, they are called neeps.

Nowadays, the confusion is not so acute. Many grocers and supermarkets sell early or baby turnips or, better still, French turnips – *navets*.

Both are small and white, tinged either with green or in the case of *navets*, with pink or purple. Consequently, people are learning to tell their rutabagas from their turnips and also discovering what a delicious vegetable the turnip is.

History

Turnips have been cultivated for centuries, principally as an important livestock feed but also for humans. Although they were not considered the food of gourmets, they have been grown by poorer families as a useful addition to the winter table.

Rutabagas were known as turnip-rooted cabbages until the 1780s, when Sweden began exporting the vegetable to Britain and the shorter name resulted.

Until recently, turnips and rutabagas have not enjoyed a very high reputation among cooks in many parts of the world. This is partly because they are perceived as cattle food and partly because few people have taken the trouble to find acceptable ways of cooking them. Many cooks tend to boil and then mash them to a watery pulp, and for many people this is the only way they have eaten either vegetable.

The French, in contrast, have had far more respect for the turnip, at least. For centuries they have devised recipes for their delicate *navets*, roasting them in, caramelizing them in sugar and butter or simply steaming and serving with butter. Young, tender turnips have also been popular all over the Mediterranean region for many years, and there are many dishes using turnips with fish, poultry, or teamed with tomatoes, onions and spinach.

Nutrition

Both turnips and rutabagas are a good source of calcium and potassium.

Varieties

French *navets*, small round, squash-shaped turnips tinged with pink or purple, are increasingly available in grocers and supermarkets in the spring. Less common, but even more prized by the French, are the long carrot-shaped turnips, called *vertus*. English turnips are generally larger and are mainly green and white. Both have the characteristic peppery flavor, but this is less pronounced in *navets* which are generally sweeter.

Rutabagas generally have a more substantial, fuller-bodied flavor than turnips but at their best have a subtle, pleasant taste. The Marian is a yellow fleshed variety with a distinct "rutabaga" flavor. White-fleshed swedes, like Merrick, have a more watery, turnip-like flavor.

Buying and Storing

Turnips: If possible, buy French *navets* or failing that, the smallest and youngest turnips, available in stores from spring. They should be firm, smooth and unblemished, ideally with fresh green tops. Store in a cool dry place.
Rutabagas: Unlike turnips, rutabagas generally seem to come large. However, if possible, choose small rutabagas with smooth and unblemished skins as large ones are likely to be tough and fibrous. Store as for turnips.

Preparing and Cooking

Turnips: Young turnips should not require peeling; simply trim, then simmer or steam until tender. They are delicious raw, thinly sliced or grated into salads.

Peel older turnips (*below*) and then slice or dice before cooking. Remember, turnips are members of the cabbage family and older specimens particularly can show signs of that unpleasant cabbage rankness if overcooked. To avoid this, blanch turnips if they are to be served as a vegetable dish, or add sparingly to soups and casseroles, so that the rank flavor is dispersed.

Rutabagas: Peel to remove the skin and then cut into chunks (*below*). Rutabagas will disintegrate if overcooked, and they are unpleasantly raw tasting if not cooked sufficiently. The only answer is to check frequently while they are cooking. Rutabagas are particularly good when teamed with other root vegetables in soups and casseroles, adding a pleasant, slightly nutty flavor.

Far left: Navets and Turnips.
Below: Rutabagas.

CARROTS

After potatoes, carrots are without doubt
our best-known and best-loved root vegetable. In the days when vegetables were
served merely as an accessory to meat,
carrots always made an appearance –
often overcooked but still eaten up
because, we were told, they helped you
to see in the dark.

Carrots have many different flavors,
depending on how they are cooked.
Young, new season carrots braised in
butter and a splash of water are intensely
flavored and sweet; when steamed, they
are tender and melting. Carrots grated
into salads are fresh and clean tasting,
while in casseroles they are savory with
the characteristic carrot flavor. In soups
they are fragrant and mild, and in cakes
their flavor can hardly be detected, yet
their sweetness adds richness.

History

Until the Middle Ages, carrots were purple. The orange carrots came from
Holland, from where they were exported
in the seventeenth and eighteenth centuries. Although purple and white carrots
continued to be eaten in France, nowadays they are something of a rarity.

Nutrition

Carrots contain large amounts of
carotene and vitamin A, along with useful amounts of vitamins B3, C and E.
When eaten raw, they also provide good
quantities of potassium, calcium, iron
and zinc, but these are reduced when
carrots are boiled.

The idea that carrots are good for your
night sight originated in the Second
World War. Early radar stations were
established along the south and east
coasts of England in 1939 to detect
aggressors in the air or at sea. The
Germans attributed this sudden remarkable night vision to the British habit of
eating carrots. Indeed, the vitamin A in
carrots forms retinal, a lack of which
brings on night blindness.

Buying and Storing

Home-grown carrots are so much nicer than shop bought ones. Almost all vegetables have a better flavor if grown organically, but this is particularly true of carrots.

When buying carrots, look out for the very young, pencil-thin ones, which are beautifully tender either eaten raw or steamed for just a few minutes. Young carrots are commonly sold with their feathery tops intact, which should be fresh and green. Older carrots should be firm and unblemished. Avoid tired looking carrots as they will have little nutritional value.

Carrots should not be stored for too long. They will keep for several days if stored in a cool, airy place or in the salad drawer of the fridge.

Preparing

Preparation depends on the age of the carrots. The valuable nutrients lie either in or just beneath the skin, so if the carrots are young, simply wash them under cold running water. Medium-size carrots may need to be scraped and large carrots will need either scraping or peeling.

Cooking

Carrots are excellent cooked or raw. Children often like raw carrots as they have a very sweet flavor. They can be cut into julienne strips, with a dressing added, or grated into salads and coleslaw – their juices run and blend wonderfully with the dressing. Carrots can be cooked in almost any way you choose. As an accompaniment, cut them into julienne strips and braise in butter and cider, or cook in the minimum of stock and toss in butter and a sprinkling of caraway seeds.

Roasted carrots are delicious, with a melt-in-the-mouth sweetness. Parboil large ones first, but younger carrots can be quickly blanched or added directly to the pan with a joint of meat.

HORSERADISH

Horseradish is grown for its pungent root, which is normally grated and mixed with cream or oil and vinegar and served with roast beef. Fresh horseradish is available in many supermarkets in the spring, and you can make your own horseradish sauce by simply peeling the root and then mixing 3 tablespoons of grated horseradish with ²/₃ cup heavy or whipping cream and adding a little Dijon mustard, vinegar and sugar to taste. As well as being excellent with hot or cold beef, horseradish sauce is delicious with smoked trout or mackerel or spread thinly on sandwiches with a fine pâté.

Left: Carrots.
Right: Horseradish.

BEETS

Experience of vinegar-sodden beets has doubtlessly put many people off them. Those who love them know to buy their beets fresh, so that they can cook them themselves. They can be served in a number of different ways: baked and served with sour cream, braised in a creamy sauce, grated in a salad or used for the classic soup *borscht*.

History

Beets are closely related to sugar beets and mangelwurzels. As the demand for sugar increased over the centuries, when sugar could successfully be extracted from beets, sugar production became a big industry in Britain and Europe.

Mangelwurzels were eaten in parts of Europe and in England in times of famine, although they were primarily grown as cattle fodder.

Beets, however, have probably been eaten since Roman times. By the mid-nineteenth century they were clearly a popular vegetable, and Mrs Beeton in her famous cookbook has 11 recipes for them, including a beet and carrot jam and beet fritters.

Nutrition

Beets are an excellent provider of potassium. The leaves, which have the flavor of spinach, are high in vitamin A, iron and calcium.

Buying and Storing

If possible, buy small beets which have their whiskers intact and have at least 2 inches of stalk at the top; if they are too closely cropped they will bleed during cooking. Beets will keep for several weeks if stored in a cool place.

Preparing

To cook beets whole, first rinse under cold running water. Cut the stalks to about 1 inch above the root and don't cut away the root or peel it – or the glorious deep red color will bleed away. When serving cold in salads, or where the recipe calls for chopped or grated beets, peel away the skin with a potato peeler or sharp knife.

Cooking

To bake in the oven, place the cleaned beet in a dish with a tight-fitting lid, and add 4-5 tablespoons of water. Lay a double layer of foil over the dish before covering with the lid, then bake in a low oven for 2-3 hours or until the beets are tender. Check occasionally to ensure the pan doesn't dry out and to see whether the beets are cooked. They are ready when the skin begins to wrinkle and can be easily rubbed away with your fingers. Alternately, simply wrap the beets in a double layer of foil and cook as above. To boil beets, prepare as above and simmer for about 1½ hours.

BEET GREENS

The tops of several root vegetables are not only edible, but are also extremely nutritious. Beet greens are particularly good, being very high in vitamins A and C, and indeed have more iron and calcium than spinach itself. They are delicious, but not easily available unless you grow your own. If you are lucky enough to get some, boil the greens for a few minutes, then drain well and serve with butter or olive oil.

Left: Beets.
Above right: Scorzonera.
Below right: Salsify.

SALSIFY <u>AND</u> SCORZONERA

These two root vegetables are closely related to each other as well as to members of the same family as dandelion and lettuce. All have long tapering roots.

Salsify has a white or pale brownish skin and scorzonera, sometimes called black salsify, has a black skin. They both have a pale creamy flesh and a fairly similar flavor reminiscent of artichokes and asparagus. Salsify is said to have the superior flavor and has been likened to oysters (it is sometimes referred to as the oyster plant), although many people fail to detect this.

Both salsify and scorzonera make an unusual and pleasant accompaniment, either creamed or fried in butter. They can also be also used in soups.

History

Salsify is native to the Mediterranean but now grows in most areas of North America and Europe. Scorzonera is a southern European plant.

Both roots are classified as herbs and, like many wild plants and herbs, their history is bound up with their use in medicines. The roots, together with their leaves and flowers, were used for the treatment of heartburn, loss of appetite and various liver diseases.

Buying and Storing

Choose specimens that are firm and smooth and, if possible, still with their tops on, which should look fresh and lively. Salsify will keep for several days stored in a cool dark place.

Preparing

Salsify and scorzonera are difficult to clean and peel. Either scrub the root under cold running water and then peel after cooking, or peel with a sharp stainless steel knife (*below*). As the flesh discolors quickly, place the trimmed pieces into acidulated water (water to which lemon juice has been added).

Cooking

Cut into short lengths and simmer for 20–30 minutes until tender. Drain well and sauté in butter, or serve with lemon juice, melted butter or chopped parsley.

Alternately, they can be puréed for soups or mashed. Cooked and cooled salsify and scorzonera can be served in a mustard or garlic vinaigrette with a simple salad.

EXOTIC ROOTS

Throughout the tropical regions of the world all sorts of tubers are grown and used for a fabulous variety of dishes. Yams, sweet potatoes, cassava and taro, to name but a few, are for many people a staple food, not only cooked whole as a vegetable accompaniment, but ground or pounded for bread and cakes. There is an enormous variety of these tropical and subtropical tubers, and while they cannot be cultivated in a moderate climate, the more common tubers are now widely available in specialist shops and in most supermarkets.

SWEET POTATOES

Sweet potatoes are another one of those vegetables that once tasted, are never forgotten. They are, as the name suggests, sweet, but they also have a slightly spicy taste. It's this distinct sweet and savory flavor which makes them such an excellent foil to many savory dishes and

they are fittingly paired with meat dishes that need a touch of sweetness, like turkey or pork.

History

Sweet potatoes are native to tropical America, but today they are grown all over the tropical world. They have been grown in South America from before the Inca civilizations and were introduced into Spain before the ordinary potato. They also have a long history of cultivation in Asia spreading from Polynesia to New Zealand in the fourteenth century.

They are an important staple food in the Caribbean and southern United States, and many famous recipes feature these vegetables. Candied sweet potatoes, for instance, are traditionally served with ham or turkey at Thanksgiving all over the United States, while Jamaica and the West Indies abound with sweet potato dishes, from the simple baked

potato to Caribbean pudding, a typically sweet and spicy dish with sweet potatoes, coconut, limes and cinnamon.

Sweet potatoes appear to have been introduced to England even earlier than regular potatoes. Henry VIII was said to have been very partial to them baked in a pie, believing they would improve his love life! If Henry VIII was eating sweet potatoes in the early/mid-sixteenth century, then it's likely he received them via the Spanish, who, thanks to Christopher Columbus, were busy conquering the New World, thus experiencing a whole range of tropical vegetables and fruit.

Varieties

The skin color ranges from white to pink to reddish brown. The red-skinned variety, which has a whitish flesh, is the one most commonly used in African and Caribbean cooking.

Buying and Storing

Choose small or medium-size ones if possible as larger specimens tend to be rather fibrous. They should be firm and evenly shaped; avoid those that seem withered, have damp patches or are sprouting. They will keep for several days in a cool place.

Preparing and Cooking

If baking, scrub the potatoes well and cook exactly as you would for ordinary potatoes. To boil, either cook in their skins and remove these after cooking, or peel and place in acidulated water (water to which lemon juice has been added). This prevents them turning brown and it's worth boiling them in lightly acidulated water for the same reason. Sweet potatoes can be cooked in any of the ways you would cook ordinary potatoes - roast, boiled, mashed or baked. However, avoid using them in creamy or gratin-type dishes. They are both too sweet and too spicy for that.

It is preferable to roast or sauté them with onions and other savory ingredients to bring out their flavor, or mash them and serve them over chunks of chicken for a crusted chicken pie.

YAMS

Yams have been a staple food for many cultures for thousands of years. There are today almost countless varieties, of different shapes, sizes and colors and called different names by different people. Most varieties are thought to have been native to China, although they found their way to Africa during a very early period and became a basic food, being easy to grow in tropical and subtropical conditions, and containing the essential carbohydrate of all staple foods.

Although cush-cush or Indian yam was indigenous to America, most yams were introduced to the New World as a result of the slave trade in the sixteenth century. Today with such a huge variety of this popular vegetable available, there are innumerable recipes for yam, many probably not printed and published, but handed down by word of mouth from mother to daughter and making their appearance at mealtimes all over the hot regions of the world.

Varieties

The greater yam, as the name suggests, can grow to a huge size. A weight of 137 pounds has been recorded. The varieties you are likely to find in stores will be about the size of a small marrow, although smaller yams are also available such as the sweet yam, which looks like a large potato and is normally covered with whiskery roots. All sizes have a coarse brown skin and can be white or red-fleshed.

In Chinese stores, you may find the Chinese yam, which is a more elongated, club-like shape and is covered with fine whiskers.

Buying

Look out for firm specimens with unbroken skins. The flesh inside should be creamy and moist and if you buy from a grocery, the storekeeper may well cut open a yam so you can check that it is fresh. They can be stored for several weeks in a cool, dark place.

Preparing

Peel away the skin thickly to remove the outer skin and the layer underneath that contains the poison dioscorine. This in fact is destroyed during cooking, but discard the peel carefully. Place the peeled yam in salted water as it discolors easily.

Cooking

Yams, like potatoes, are used as the main starchy element in a meal, boiled and mashed, fried, sautéed or roasted. They tend to have an affinity with spicy sauces and are delicious cut into discs, fried and sprinkled with a little salt and cayenne pepper. African cooks frequently pound boiled yam to make a dough which is then served with spicy stews and soups.

TARO/EDDO

Like yams, taro is another hugely important tuber in tropical areas, and for thousands of years it has been a staple food for many people. It goes under many different names; in South-east Asia, South and Central America, all over Africa and in the Caribbean it is called variously eddo and dasheen.

There are two basic varieties of taro – a large barrel-shaped tuber and a smaller variety, which is often called eddo or dasheen. They are all a dark mahogany brown with a rather shaggy skin, looking like a cross between a beet and a rutabaga.

Although they look very similar, taro belongs to a completely different family from yam and in flavor and texture is noticeably different. Boiled, it has a completely unique flavor, something like a floury water chestnut.

Buying and Storing

Try to buy small specimens; the really small smooth bulbs are tiny attachments to the larger taro and are either called eddoes, or rather sweetly, "sons of taro." Stored in a cool, dark place, they should keep for several weeks.

Left: Sweet potatoes.
Above: Yams.

Preparing

Taros, like yams, contain a poison just under the skin which produces an allergic reaction. Consequently, either peel taros thickly, wearing rubber gloves, or cook in their skins. The toxins are completely eliminated by boiling, and the skins peel off easily.

Cooking

Taros soak up large quantities of liquid during cooking, and this can be turned to advantage by cooking in well-flavored stock or with tomatoes and other vegetables. For this reason, they are excellent in soups and casseroles, adding bulk and flavor in a similar way to potatoes. They can also be steamed or boiled, deep-fried or puréed for fritters, but must be served hot as they become sticky if allowed to cool.

CALLALOO

Callaloo are the leaves of the taro plant, poisonous if eaten raw, but used widely in Asian and Caribbean recipes. They are cooked thoroughly, then used for wrapping meat and vegetables. Callaloo can also be shredded and cooked together with pork, bacon, crab, shrimp, okra, chili, onions and garlic, together with lime and coconut milk to make one of the Caribbean's most famous dishes, named after the leaves themselves, Callaloo.

JICAMA

Also known as the Mexican potato, this large root vegetable is a native of central America. It has a thin brown skin and white, crunchy flesh which has a sweet, nutty taste. It can be eaten cooked in the same way as potatoes or sliced and added raw to salads.

Buy specimens that are firm to the touch. Jicama in good condition will keep for about two weeks if stored in a plastic bag in the refrigerator.

Top: Taros (Eddoes).
Above: Jicama.
Left: Callaloo.

CASSAVA

This is another very popular West Indian root, used in numerous Caribbean dishes. It is native to Brazil, and found its way to the West Indies surprisingly via Africa, where it also became a popular vegetable. Known as cassava in the West Indies, it is called manioc or mandioc in Brazil, and juca or yucca is used in other parts of South America.

Cassava is used to make tapioca, and in South America a sauce and an intoxicating beverage are prepared from the juice. However, in Africa and the West Indies it is eaten as a vegetable either boiled, baked or fried, or cooked and pounded to a dough to make *fufu,* a traditional savory African pudding.

Right: Cassava.
Below left: Ginger.
Below right: Galangal.

GINGER <u>AND</u> GALANGAL

GINGER

This is probably the world's most important and popular spice and is associated with a number of different cuisines - Chinese, Indian and Caribbean, to name but a few. It was known in Europe during the Roman period, but was still fairly rare until the spice routes opened up trade in the sixteenth and seventeenth centuries. Like many spices, ginger has the quality of enhancing and complementing both sweet and savory food, adding a fragrant spiciness to all sorts of dishes. However, while ground ginger is best in recipes which will be baked, and preserved ginger, where the ginger is preserved in syrup, tastes wonderful in desserts, for savory dishes, always use fresh ginger.

Nowadays, the pale, knobbly roots of fresh ginger are widely available in supermarkets and whenever possible, buy just a small quantity, as you will not need a great deal and fresh ginger will not keep indefinitely.

To prepare, simply peel away the skin with a sharp knife and grate or thinly slice according to the recipe.

GREATER GALANGAL

Galangal looks similar to ginger except that the rhizome is thinner and the young shoots are bright pink. The roots should be prepared in the same way as ginger and can be used in curries and satay sauces.

— FOUR —
GREENS

Spinach

Brussels Sprouts

Cauliflower

Sprouting Broccoli
and Calabrese

Turnip Tops

Cabbage

Kale and Curly Kale

Garden and Wild Leaves

Chinese Greens

Kohlrabi

Chard

SPINACH

For many people, spinach is inextricably linked with Popeye, the cartoon character who used to eat huge amounts of spinach. It is a wonderfully versatile vegetable, popular worldwide, with nearly every cuisine featuring spinach somewhere in its repertoire. The Italians are particularly partial to spinach and have hundreds of dishes using the vegetable. The words *à la florentine* mean the dish contains spinach.

As well as being delicious on its own, chopped or puréed spinach can be mixed with a range of other ingredients with superb results. It has a particular affinity with dairy products and in the Middle East, feta or helim cheese is used to make boreks or other spinach pies. The Italians mix spinach with ricotta or Parmesan cheese for a huge range of recipes, and the English use eggs and sometimes Cheddar for a spinach soufflé.

History

Spinach was first cultivated in Persia several thousands of years ago. It came to Europe via the Arab world; the Moors introduced it to Spain, and Arabs in the Middle East took it to Greece. It first appeared in England in the fourteenth century, probably via Spain. It is mentioned in the first known English cookbook, where it is referred to as *spynoches*, which echoes the Spanish word for spinach, *espinacas*. It quickly became a popular vegetable, probably because it is quick and easy to grow and similarly easy and quick to cook.

Nutrition

Spinach is an excellent source of vitamin C if eaten raw, as well as vitamins A and B, calcium, potassium and iron. Spinach was originally thought to provide far more iron than it actually does, but the iron is "bound" up by oxalic acid in cooked spinach, which prevents the body absorbing anything but the smallest amounts. Even so, it is still an extremely healthy vegetable whether eaten cooked or raw.

Buying and Storing

Spinach grows all year through, so you should have no difficulty in buying it fresh. Frozen spinach is a poor substitute, mainly because it has so little flavor, so it is worth the effort to use the fresh product.

Spinach leaves should be green and lively; if they look tired and the stalks are floppy, shop round until you find something in better condition. Spinach reduces significantly when cooked: about 1 pound will serve two people. Store it in the salad drawer of the fridge, where it will keep for 1-2 days.

Preparing

Wash well in a bowl of cold water and remove any tough or large stalks.

Cooking

Throw the leaves into a large pan with just the water that clings to the leaves and place over a low heat with a sprinkling of salt. Cover the pan so the spinach steams in its own liquid and shake the pan occasionally to prevent the spinach sticking to the bottom. It cooks in 4-6 minutes, wilting down to about an eighth of its former volume. Drain and press out the remaining liquid with the back of a spoon.

Spinach can be used in a variety of ways. It can be chopped and served with lots of butter, or similarly served with other spring vegetables such as

BRUSSELS SPROUTS

baby carrots or young fava beans. For frittatas, chop the spinach finely, stir in a little Parmesan cheese, a good sprinkling of salt and pepper and a dash of cream, if liked, and stir into the omelet before cooking. Alternately, purée it for sauces or blend it for soups. Spinach is also delicious raw, served with chopped bacon or croûtons. A fresh spinach salad is delicious as the leaves have just the right balance of flavor – sharp but not overpowering.

Below: Spinach.
Below right: Brussels sprouts.

Brussels sprouts have a pronounced and sweet nutty flavor, quite unlike cabbage, although the two are closely related. They are traditionally served at Christmas with chestnuts and indeed have a definite affinity for certain nuts – particularly the sweet flavored nuts, e.g. almonds, pair well rather than hazelnuts or walnuts.

History

Brussels sprouts were cultivated in Flanders (now Belgium) during the Middle Ages. They are basically miniature cabbages which grow in a knobbly row on a long tough stalk. The Germans call sprouts *rosenkohl* – rose cabbage – a pretty and descriptive name as they look like small rosebuds.

Buying and Storing

Buy Brussels sprouts as fresh as possible as older ones are more likely to have that strong unpleasant "cabbage" flavor. They should be small and hard with tightly wrapped leaves. Avoid any that are turning yellow or brown or have loose leaves.

Brussels sprouts will keep for several days in a cool place such as a larder or salad drawer of a fridge, but it is far better to buy them as you need them.

Preparing

Cut away the bottom of the stalk and remove the outer leaves. Some people cut a cross through the bottom of the stalk although this is not really necessary. If you haven't been able to avoid buying big Brussels sprouts, cut them in half or into quarters, or slice them thinly for stir-frying.

Cooking

As with cabbage, either cook Brussels sprouts very briefly or braise slowly in the oven. Cook in small amounts of fast boiling water for about 3 minutes until just tender. To stir-fry Brussels sprouts, slice into three or four pieces and then fry in a little oil and butter – they taste great with onions and ginger.

CAULIFLOWER

Cauliflower is a member of the cabbage family, *Brassica oleracea*. Like all cabbages, cauliflower suffers terribly from overcooking. A properly cooked cauliflower has a pleasant fresh flavor but when overcooked it turns grey and becomes unpalatably soft, taking on a nasty rank flavor with an unpleasant aftertaste. Children often like raw cauliflower even though they may not connect it with the same vegetable served up as boiled.

History

Cauliflower is thought to have come orig-inally from China and thence to the Middle East. The Moors introduced it to Spain in the twelfth century and from there it found its way to England via established trading routes. The early cauliflower was the size of a tennis ball but is has gradually been cultivated to the enormous sizes we see today. Ironically, baby cauliflowers are now fashionable.

Varieties

Green and occasionally purple cauli-flowers are available in the stores. The purple variety was originally grown in Sardinia and Italy but is increasingly grown by other market gardeners. They look pretty and unusual but are other-wise similar to white cauliflower. Dwarf varieties of cauliflower are now common-ly available in stores.

Broccoli Romanescoes: As well as baby white cauliflowers, broccoli romanescoes are also avaliable.These pretty green or white vegetables look like a cross between broccoli and cauliflower, but are more closely related to cauliflower. They taste very much like cauliflower, but since they are quite small, they are less likely to be overcooked and consequently retain their excellent flavor.

Broccoflower: A cross between broccoli and cauliflower, this looks like a pale green cauliflower. It has a mild flavor and should be cooked in the same way as you would cauliflower.

Right: Baby cauliflowers.
Far right top: Broccoli romanescoes.
Far right bottom: Green cauliflowers.

Nutrition

Cauliflower contains potassium, iron and zinc, although cooking reduces the amounts. It is also a good source of vitamins A and C.

Buying and Storing

In top condition, a cauliflower is a creamy white color with the outer leaves curled round the flower. The head should be unblemished with no black or discolored areas and the outer leaves should look fresh and crisp. Keep cauliflower in a cool place for no longer than 1-2 days; after that it will deteriorate and valuable nutrients will be lost.

Preparing

To cook a cauliflower whole, first trim away the coarse bottom leaves (leave the inner ones on, if liked). Very large cauliflowers are best halved or broken into florets, as the outside will overcook before the inside is tender. Some people trim away the stalk, but others like this part and only trim off the very thick stalk at the bottom of the plant.

Cooking

Cauliflowers are excellent steamed, either whole or in florets. Place in a steamer or colander over a pan of boiling water, cover and steam until just tender and immediately remove from the heat. The florets can then be fried in olive oil or butter for a few minutes to give a lightly browned finish.

When cooking a cauliflower whole, start testing it after 10 minutes; it should feel tender but still have plenty of "bite" left in it. Cauliflower is a popular vegetable accompaniment, either served with just a little butter, or with a tomato or cheese sauce. It is also good stir-fried with onions and garlic together with a few tomatoes and capers.

Cauliflower is excellent in salads or used for crudités. Either use it raw or blanch it in boiling water for 1-2 minutes, then refresh under cold running water.

Small cauliflowers and broccoli romanescoes are intended to be cooked whole, and can be steamed or boiled, covered with a lid, in the minimum of water for 4-5 minutes until just tender.

SPROUTING BROCCOLI AND CALABRESE

Varieties

Calabrese Broccoli: This is the vegetable we today commonly call broccoli, with large beautiful, blue-green heads on succulent stalks. It is named after the Italian province of Calabria where this variety was first developed.

Purple Sprouting Broccoli: The original variety – it has long thin stalks with small flowerheads that are normally purple but can be white or green. Heads, stalks and tender leaves are all edible. The purple heads turn green when cooked but the others keep their color. Purple sprouting broccoli is more seasonal than the easily available calabrese; it is usually available from late winter onward.

Buying and Storing

If possible, buy loose broccoli rather than the pre-wrapped bundles, because it is easier to check that it is fresh and also because wrapped vegetables tend to deteriorate more quickly.

Purple sprouting broccoli can also be sold loose or prepacked. Check that the stalk, flower head and leaves all look fresh and that the florets are tightly closed and bright green. Neither type will keep for long.

Broccoli or calabrese is a relatively modern vegetable and is one of the most popular. It is quick and easy to prepare with little or no waste and similarly easy to cook. It is attractive, whether served raw or cooked, and you can buy it in the quantity you require, unlike cauliflower or cabbage.

History

Before calabrese came into our stores, people bought and ate purple sprouting broccoli. This is basically an "untidy" version of calabrese, with long shoots and clusters of flowerheads at the end – the broccoli we know today has neat tidy heads. The stalks of purple sprouting broccoli have a faint asparagus flavor.

The Romans cooked purple sprouting broccoli in wine or served it with sauces and it is still a popular vegetable today in Italy, cooked in the oven with anchovies and onions or served with pasta in a garlic and tomato sauce.

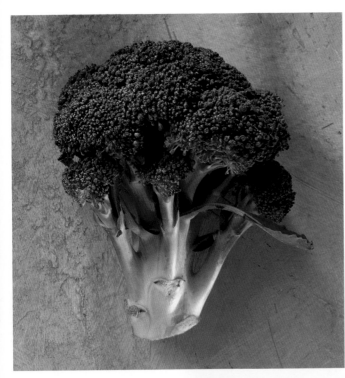

Preparing and Cooking

Trim the ends and remove any discolored leaves.

Calabrese Broccoli: Break into even-size pieces, dividing the stem and floret lengthwise if they are thick. Cook in a little boiling water for 4-5 minutes until just tender and then drain. Do not steam this variety of broccoli as its vibrant green color tends to turn gray.

Purple Sprouting Broccoli: Either steam in long, even-size lengths in a steamer or, if you have an asparagus steamer, cook as you would asparagus. Alternately, tie the stems loosely together and stand in a little water – if necessary, wedge it in with a potato or rolled up piece of foil. Cover with a dome of foil and steam for 4-5 minutes until tender.

Serving

Serve both varieties simply with butter and lemon juice or with a hollandaise or béarnaise sauce as an accompaniment. They are also excellent stir-fried.

Above far left: Purple cauliflower.
Below far left: Purple sprouting broccoli.
Above: Calabrese broccoli.
Below: Turnip tops.

TURNIP TOPS

Turnip tops, like beet greens, are both delicious and nutritious. They are not widely available but if you are able to buy some or if you grow your own, slice them *(below)* and boil or steam for a few minutes, then drain and serve with butter.

CABBAGE

Cabbage, sliced and cooked, can be one of two things: deliciously crisp, with a mild pleasant flavor – or overcooked and horrible! Cabbage and other brassicas contain the chemical hydrogen sulphide, which is activated during cooking at about the point the vegetable starts to soften. It eventually disappears, but during the in-between time, cabbage acquires its characteristic rank smell and flavor. So, either cook cabbage briefly, or cook it long and slow, preferably with other ingredients so that flavors can mingle.

History

Cabbage has a long and varied history. However, because there are many varieties of cabbage under the general heading of "brassica", it is difficult to be sure whether the variety the Greeks and Romans enjoyed is the same as today's round cabbage, or something more akin to kale or even Chinese cabbage.

The round cabbages we know today were an important food during the Dark Ages, and by the Middle Ages they were in abundance, as you will see if you study the paintings of that period. These commonly show kitchen tables or baskets at market positively groaning with fruit and vegetables, and cabbages in all their shapes and sizes were often featured.

Medieval recipes suggest cooking cabbages with leeks, onions and herbs. In the days when all except the very wealthy cooked everything in one pot, it is fair to assume that cabbages were cooked long and slow.

Varieties

Savoy Cabbage: This is a variety of green cabbage with crimped or curly leaves. It has a mild flavor and is particularly tender, thus needing less cooking than other varieties.
Spring Greens: These have fresh loose heads with a pale yellow-green heart. They are available in spring and are delicious simply sliced, steamed and served with butter.

Right: Savoy cabbage.
Above far right: Green cabbage.
Below far right: Spring greens.

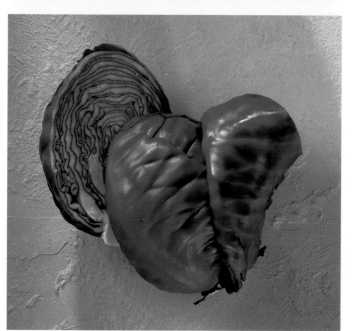

Green Cabbage: The early green, or spring, cabbages are dark green, loose-leafed and have a slightly pointed head. They have little or no heart as they are picked before this has had time to develop. Nevertheless, they are a very good cabbage and all but the very outside leaves should be tender. As the season progresses, larger, firmer and more pale green cabbages are available. These are a little tougher than the spring cabbages and need longer cooking.

Red Cabbage: A beautifully colored cabbage with smooth firm leaves. The color fades during cooking unless a little vinegar is added to the water. Red cabbage can be pickled or stewed with spices and flavorings.

White Cabbage: Sometimes called Dutch cabbages, white cabbages have smooth firm pale green leaves. They are available throughout the winter. They are good cooked or raw. To cook, slice them thinly, then boil or steam and serve with butter. To serve raw, slice thinly and use in a coleslaw.

Buying and Storing

Cabbages should be fresh looking and unblemished. When buying, avoid any with wilted leaves or those that look or feel puffy. Savoys and collard greens will keep in a cool place for several days; firmer cabbages will keep happily for much longer.

Preparing

Remove the outer leaves, if necessary, and then cut into quarters. Remove the stalk and then slice or shred according to your recipe or to taste.

Cooking

For green or white cabbages, place the shredded leaves in a pan with a pat of butter and a couple of tablespoons of water to prevent burning. Cover and cook over a medium heat until the leaves are tender, occasionally shaking the pan or stirring.

Red cabbage is cooked quite differently and is commonly sautéed in oil or butter and then braised in a low oven for up to $1^1/_2$ hours with apples, currants, onions, vinegar, wine, sugar and spices.

KALE AND CURLY KALE

Kale is the name used for a variety of green-leafed vegetables of the brassica family. Most kales have thick stems and robust leaves that do not form a head. Many kales have curly leaves, which are the variety most commonly eaten. Large coarse-leafed kales are grown for cattle and sheep feeds.

History

Kale is thought to be one of the first cultivated brassicas. Colewort, the wild ancestor, still grows along the coasts of western Europe.

Varieties

Collards: Collards, or collard greens, are a popular green vegetable in the southern United States. They are grown in summer and autumn for harvesting in the spring and are a good source of vitamin A.

Curly Kale: With its crimped, curly leaves, this is the most commonly available kale, although even this can be quite hard to come by. If you are a big fan and don't grow your own, try farm stores in early spring.

Purple or Silver Kale: This is an ornamental variety, and is grown almost exclusively for display.

Preparing and Cooking

Kale is probably the strongest tasting of the brassicas and is best cooked simply, paired with a bland-flavored vegetable, such as potatoes. To prepare, break the leaves from the stalk and then cut out any thick stalk from the leaf. This can then be rolled and sliced or cooked whole. Boil the leaves in a little salted water for 3-5 minutes until tender. Owing to its robust nature, kale is frequently teamed with fairly hot spices and is consequently popular in many Indian dishes.

Above far left: White cabbage.
Below far left: Red cabbage.
Left: Collards.
Above: Curly kale.

CHINESE GREENS

CHINESE CABBAGE/LEAVES (PE-TSAI)

Chinese cabbage, also called Napa cabbage, has pale green, crinkly leaves with long, wide, white ribs. Its shape is a little like a very fat head of celery, which gives rise to another of its alternative names, celery cabbage. It is pleasantly crunchy with a faint cabbage flavor, and, since it is available all year through, it makes a useful winter salad component. Chinese cabbage is also very good stir-fried with a tasty sauce. It is an essential ingredient of many oriental recipes.

Buying and Storing

For some reason, Chinese leaves almost always look fresh and perky when on sale in the supermarket, which probably indicates that they travel well and are transported quickly. Avoid any with discoloured or damaged stems. The leaves should be pale green and straight without blemishes or bruises. They will keep for up to six days in the salad drawer of the fridge.

Preparing

Remove the outside leaves and slice as much as you need.

Many Chinese greens are members of the brassica family. If you go into a popular and reasonably large Chinese supermarket, you'll be astonished at the varieties of green vegetables for sale. Discovering the names of these vegetables, on the other hand, can be a bit of a hit-and-miss undertaking, as the store-keepers, although always well intentioned, rarely know the English name, if indeed there is one.

CHINESE MUSTARD GREENS

Mustard greens are worth buying if you can, as they are very good to eat. The plant is a member of the cabbage family, but is grown in Europe solely for its mustard seed. In India and Asia it has long been grown for its oil seed, but the Chinese developed the plant for its leaves as well. These are deep green and slightly puckered-looking and have a definite mustard flavor, which can be quite fiery.

If you grow your own, then you'll be able to enjoy the young leaves which can be added to lettuce to spice up salads. Older leaves are best stir-fried and then dressed with a light Chinese sauce. They are also good cooked with onion and garlic and served as a side dish to accompany pork or bacon.

Preparing and Cooking

Break apart the stalks, rinse, then cut both stalks and leaves into thick or thin slices. These can then be stir-fried with garlic and onions, or cooked and served as you would chard. It has a pleasant flavor, milder than mustard greens, yet with more bite than the bland Chinese cabbage.

CHINESE BROCCOLI

This is another leafy vegetable, but with slender heads of flowers that look a little like our own broccoli, except that the flowers are usually white or yellow. Once the thicker stalks are trimmed, the greens can be sliced and cooked and served in the same way as Chinese mustard greens.

Far left: Chinese mustard greens.
Left: Chinese leaves.
Above: Chinese broccoli.
Below: Pak-choi.

Cooking and Serving

If adding to salads, combine Chinese cabbage with something fairly forceful, like Belgian endive or arugula, and add a well-flavored dressing. If adding to a stir-fry, cook with garlic, ginger and other fairly strong flavors. While the faint cabbage flavor will be lost, you will still get the pleasant crunchy "bite" of the stalk, and the leaves will carry the sauce.

PAK-CHOI

If you frequent your local Chinese super-market, you will almost certainly have come across *Pak-Choi*. In English it should correctly be called Chinese celery cabbage and its thick stalks, joined at the end in a small root, are vaguely celery-like. Its leaves, on the other hand, are generally large and spoon shaped. There are many different species of this vegetable, and smaller specimens look more like the tops of radishes and have small slim stalks. Consequently the vegetable can be known by all sorts of picturesque names, like "horse's ear" and "horse's tail." There's no rule for discovering exactly what you are buying, but the important thing is to choose a fresh plant whatever its size: look for fresh green leaves and crisp stalks.

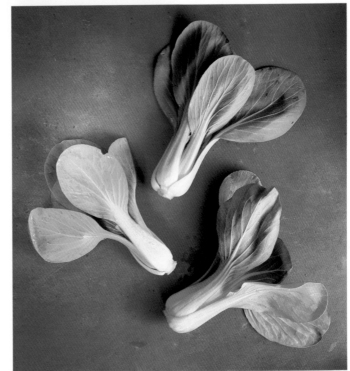

KOHLRABI

Kohlrabi looks like a cross between a cabbage and a turnip and is often classified as a root vegetable, even though it grows above ground. It is a member of the brassica family, but, unlike cabbages, it is the bulbous stalk that is edible rather than the flowering heads.

There are two varieties of kohlrabi: one is purple and the other pale green. They both have the same mild and fresh tasting flavor, not dissimilar to water chestnuts. Kohlrabi is neither as peppery as turnip nor as distinctive as cabbage, but it is easy to see why people think it a little like both. It can be served as an alternative to carrots or turnips.

History

Although kohlrabi is not a very popular vegetable in North America, it is commonly eaten in Europe, as well as in China, India and Asia. In Kashmir, where it is grown, there are many recipes – the bulbs are often finely sliced and eaten in salads and the greens are cooked in mustard oil with garlic and chilies.

Buying and Storing

Kohlrabi is best when small and young, since larger specimens tend to be coarse and fibrous. It keeps well for 7-10 days if stored in a cool place.

Preparing

Peel the skin with a knife and then cook whole or slice.

Cooking

Very small kohlrabies are tender and can be cooked whole. However, if they are any bigger than 2 inches in diameter, they can be stuffed. To do this, hollow out a little before cooking and then stuff with fried onions and tomatoes, for instance. For sliced kohlrabi, cook until just tender and serve with butter or a creamy sauce. They can also be cooked long and slow in gratin dishes, with, for instance, potatoes as a variation of *gratin Dauphinois*. Alternately, parboil them and bake in the oven covered with a cheese sauce.

CHARD

Chard is one of those vegetables that needs plenty of water when growing, which explains why it is a popular garden vegetable in many places which have a high rainfall. Gardeners are very fond of chard, not only because it is delicious to eat but also because it is so very striking.

Chard is often likened to spinach. The leaves have similarities, although they are not related and chard is on an altogether larger scale. Chard leaves are large and fleshy with distinctive white ribs, and the flavor is stronger and more robust than spinach. It is popular in France where it is baked with rice, eggs and milk in *tians*, and cooked in a celebrated pastry from Nice – *tourte de blettes* – which is a sweet tart filled with raisins, pine nuts, apples and chard bound together with eggs. It is also often combined with eggs in frittatas and tortillas.

Chard is a member of the beet family and is called by several names on this theme, including sea kale beet and spinach beet.

Ruby or rhubarb chard has striking red ribs and leaf beet is often cultivated as a decorative plant, but they both have the same flavor, and unlike sugar beet and beets, they are cultivated only for their leaves.

Buying and Storing

Heads of chard should be fresh and bright green; avoid those with withered leaves or flabby stems. It keeps better than spinach but should be eaten within a couple of days.

Preparing

Some people buy or grow chard for the white stems alone and discard the leaves (or give them to pet guinea pigs), but this is a waste of a delicious vegetable. The leaf needs to be separated from the ribs, and this can be done roughly with a sharp knife (*right*) or more precisely using scissors. The ribs can then be sliced. Either shred the leaves, or blanch them and use them to wrap little parcels of fragrant rice or other food. If the chard is young and small, the ribs do not need to be removed.

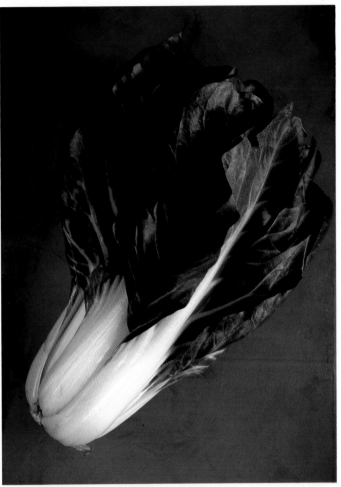

Cooking

For pies, frittatas and gratins, the leaves and ribs can be cooked together. Gently sauté the ribs in butter and oil and then add the leaves a minute or so later. Alternately, the ribs can be simmered in a little water until tender and the leaves added a few minutes later or steamed over the top.

Above far left: Kohlrabi.
Left: Purple kohlrabi.
Above: Chard.

BEANS,
PEAS
AND
SEEDS

Fava Beans

Wax Beans

Peas

Green Beans

Corn

Okra

Dried Beans and Peas

FAVA BEANS

One of the delights of having a garden is discovering how truly delicious some vegetables are when garden fresh. This seems particularly true of fava beans, which have a superb sweet flavor that sadly can never be reproduced in the frozen product. If you're lucky enough to grow or be given fresh fava beans, don't worry about recipes; just cook them until tender and serve with butter. It will be a revelation! However, if you're not one of those lucky few, don't dismiss fava beans, as they are still a wonderfully versatile vegetable. They can be used in soups or casseroles, and, since they have a mealy texture, they also purée well.

History

People have been eating fava beans almost since time began. A variety of wild fava bean grew all over southern Europe, North Africa and Asia, and it would have been a useful food for early man. There is archaeological evidence that by Neolithic times fava beans were being farmed, making them one of the first foods to be cultivated.

Fava beans will grow in most climates and most soils. They were a staple food for people throughout the Dark Ages and the Middle Ages, grown for feeding people and livestock until being replaced by the potato in the seventeenth and eighteenth centuries. Fava beans were an important source of protein for the poor, and because they dry well, they would have provided nourishing meals for families until the next growing season.

Nutrition

Beans are high in protein and carbohydrates and are also a good source of vitamins A, B1 and B2. They also provide potassium and iron as well as several other minerals.

Buying and Storing

Buy beans as fresh as possible. The pods should preferably be small and tender. Use as soon as possible.

Preparing

Very young beans in tender pods, no more than 3 inches in length, can be eaten pod and all; top and tail, and then slice roughly. Usually, however, you will need to shell the beans. Elderly beans are often better skinned after they are cooked to rid them of the strong, bitter flavor that puts many people off this vegetable.

Cooking

Plunge shelled beans (or in their pods if very young) into rapidly boiling water and cook until just tender. They can also be parboiled and then finished off braised in butter. For a simple broad bean purée, blend the cooked beans with garlic cooked in butter, cream and a pinch of fresh herbs, such as savory or thyme.

LIMA BEANS

These are popular in the US, named after the capital of Peru, and are sold mainly shelled. They are an essential ingredient in the Native American dish *succotash*. Lima beans should be cooked in a little boiling water until tender. Elderly beans need skinning after they are cooked. The dried bean, also known as the butter bean, can be large or small. These large beans tend to become mushy when cooked so are best used in soups or purées.

Above: Fava beans.
Below: Lima beans.
Right: Wax beans.

WAX BEANS

The wax bean is native to South America, where it has been cultivated for more than 2000 years, and there is archaeological evidence of its existence much earlier than that.

It is a popular vegetable to grow. Most home vegetable gardeners have a patch of wax beans – they are easy to grow and, like all legumes, their roots contain bacteria that help renew nitrogen supplies in the soil.

They have a more robust flavor and texture than French beans and are distinct from green beans in several ways: they are generally much larger with long, flattened pods; their skin is rough textured, although in young beans this softens during cooking; and they contain purple beans within the pods, unlike green beans whose beans are mostly white or pale green. Nevertheless, runner beans belong to the same family as all the green beans.

Buying and Storing

Always buy young beans as the pods of larger beans are likely to be tough. The pods should feel firm and fresh; if you can see the outline of the bean inside the pod it is likely to be fibrous – although you could leave the beans to dry out and use the dried beans later in the season. Ideally, the beans inside should be no larger than your small fingernail.

Use as soon as possible after buying; they do not store well.

Preparing

Wax beans need to be topped and tailed and may also need stringing. Carefully put your knife through the top of the bean without cutting right through, and then pull downward; if a thick thread comes away, the beans need stringing, so do the same on the other side. The beans can then be sliced either using a sharp knife or a slicer.

Slice through lengthwise, not diagonally, so that you will be able to serve the beans with just a little skin and lots of succulent flesh.

Cooking

Plunge the beans into boiling salted water and cook until *al dente*.

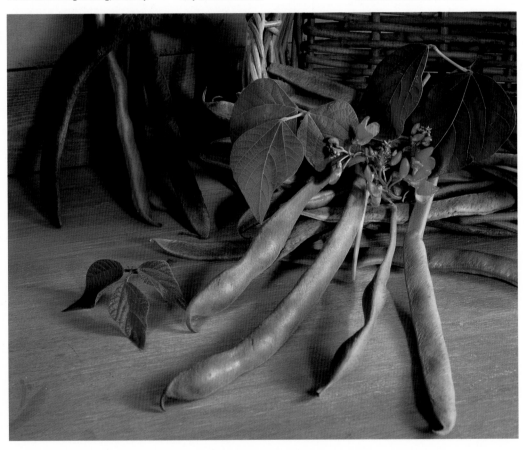

PEAS

Fresh peas are wonderful – try tasting them raw, straight from the pod. Unfortunately, the season for garden peas is short, and frozen peas, which are the next best thing, never quite come up to the mark. If you grow your own peas, for three or four weeks in early summer, you can eat like a king; otherwise you can buy them from a good grocer, who may be able to keep you supplied all through the early summer.

History

Peas have an even longer history than fava beans, with archaeological evidence showing they were cultivated as long ago as 5700 BC. High in protein and carbohydrates, they would have been another important staple food and were eaten fresh or dried for soups or potage.

"Pease" porridge is mentioned in a Greek play written in 5 BC. "Pease pudding," probably something similar, made with split peas with onion and herbs, is an old-fashioned but still very popular dish, especially in the north of England, traditionally eaten with ham and pork.

One of the first recipes for peas, however, comes from *Le Cuisinier Français*, which was translated into English in the middle of the seventeenth century and gives a recipe for *petits pois à la française* (peas cooked with small-hearted lettuces) – still a popular recipe today.

Varieties

Snow peas: These are eaten whole and have a delicate flavor, providing they are not overcooked. Unfortunately, they are easy to overcook and the texture then becomes rather slippery. Alternately, blanch or stir-fry them. They are also good served raw in salads.

Petits Pois: These are not, as you might expect, immature peas but are a dwarf variety. Gardeners grow their own, but they are not available fresh in the stores as they are mainly grown commercially for canning or freezing.

Sugar Peas, Sugar Snaps: These have the distinct fresh flavor of raw peas and are more plump and have more snap than snow peas.

Buying and Storing

Only buy fresh peas; if they are old they are bound to be disappointing and you would be better off buying them frozen. In top condition, the pods are bright green and lively looking; the more withered the pod, the longer they have been hanging around. It is possible to surreptitiously sample peas on occasion, to check if they are fresh (grocers don't seem to mind if you buy some). Use fresh peas as soon as possible.

Preparing

Shelling peas can be very relaxing. Press open the pods and use your thumb to push out the peas *(below)*. Snow peas and sugar snaps just need to be topped and tailed *(below right)*.

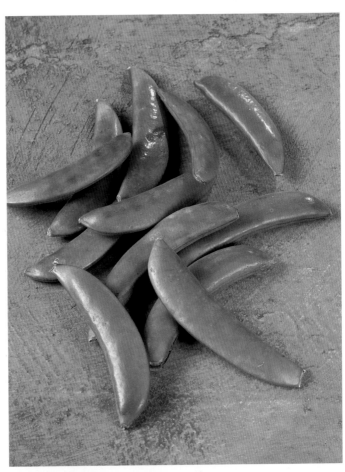

Cooking

Cook peas with a sprig of mint in a pan of rapidly boiling water or in a covered steamer until tender. Alternately, melt butter in a flameproof casserole, add the peas and then cover and sweat over low heat for 4–5 minutes. Cook snow peas and sugar snaps in any of these ways but for a shorter time.

Left: Peas.
Above right: Sugar snap peas.

GREEN BEANS

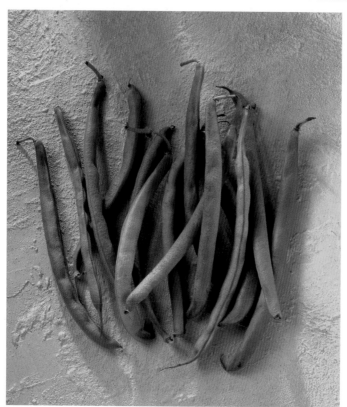

Whether you call beans French beans, haricots or green beans, they all belong to a large and varied family.

History

The bean is a New World vegetable that had been cultivated for thousands of years by native peoples in both the north and south of the continent, which accounts for its wide diversity.

Varieties

One variety or another is available all year through and so they are one of the most convenient fresh green vegetables.
French Beans: This name encompasses a range of green beans, including the snap bean and bobby bean. They are mostly fat and fleshy, and when fresh, should be firm so that they break in half with a satisfying snapping sound.

Haricots Verts: These are considered the best French beans and are delicate and

slim in shape. They should be eaten when very young, no more than 2½-3 inches in length.
Thai Beans: These long beans are similar to French beans and can be prepared and cooked in the same way.
Yellow Wax Beans: This is also a French bean and has a mild, slightly buttery taste.

Buying and Storing

Whatever variety, beans should be bright and crisp. Avoid wilted ones, or those with overly mature pods which feel spongy when lightly squeezed. They do not keep well, so use as soon as possible after buying or picking.

Preparing

To remove the ends of the beans: gather them together in one hand and then slice away the top ¼ inch *(below)*, then do the same at the other end. If necessary, pull off any stringy bits.

Cooking

Plunge beans into rapidly boiling salted water and cook until *al dente*. When overcooked, beans have a flabby texture and also lose much of their flavor. Drain and toss them in butter or serve in a sauce with shallots and bacon. For salads, cook until just tender and then refresh under cold water. They are excellent with a garlicky vinaigrette. Serve with carrots or other root vegetables and savor the contrast in flavors.

Above left: Bobby beans.
Below left: Yellow wax beans.
Right: Haricots verts.
Below: Thai beans.

CORN

Fresh corn, eaten on the cob with salt
and a little butter, is deliciously sweet.
Some gardeners who grow it have a pan
ready on the boil, so that when they cut
the corn it goes into the pan in only the
time it takes to race up from the garden
to the kitchen. Buying it from the
supermarket is inevitably a bit hit-or-
miss, although if purchased in season,
corn can be very good indeed.

History

In 1492, as Christopher Columbus
disembarked on the island now called
Cuba, he was met by Native Americans
offering two gifts of hospitality – one was
tobacco and the other something the
Native Americans called *maïs*. The
English word for staple food was then
corn, so that when Columbus and his
crew saw that maize was the staple food
for the Native Americans, it was dubbed
"Indian corn."

Corn originated in South America and
had enormous significance to the Native
Americans of the whole continent, who
were said to have lived and died by corn.
They referred to it as their "first mother and
father, the source of life." By far their most
important food, corn was used in many
other ways as well. They used the plant for
their shelters and for fences, and they wore
it and decorated their bodies with it.

The Aztecs had corn planting
ceremonies that included human
sacrifices, and other tribes had similar
customs to appease the god "corn."
Countless myths and legends have been
woven around corn, each tribe telling a
slightly different story, but each on the
same theme of planting and harvesting
corn. For anthropologists and historians,
they make compelling study.

Nutrition

Corn is a good carbohydrate food and is
rich in vitamins A, B and C. It contains
protein, but less so than most other
cereals. It is also a good source of potassium, magnesium, phosphorus and iron.

Varieties

There are five main varieties of corn –
popcorn, sweet corn, dent corn, flint
corn and flour corn. Dent corn is the

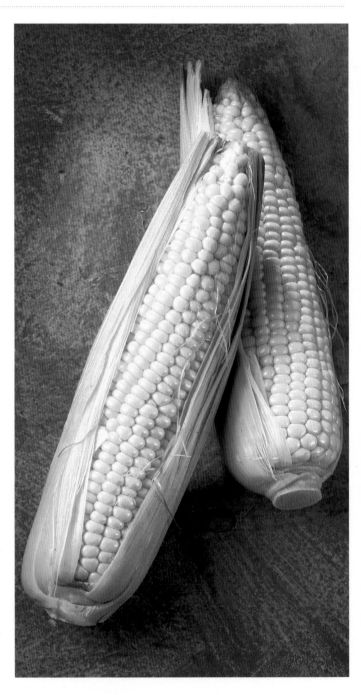

most commonly grown worldwide, for animal feeds and oil, and the corn we eat on the cobs is sweet corn. Baby corn cobs are picked when immature and are cooked and eaten whole.

Buying and Storing

As soon as corn is picked, its sugar begins to turn to starch and therefore the sooner it goes into the pot, the better. Wherever possible, buy locally grown corn.

Look for husks that are clean and green and tassels which are golden, with no sign of matting. The corn itself should look plump and yellow. Avoid cobs with pale or white kernels or those with older shriveled kernels which will undoubtedly be disappointing.

Preparing

Strip away the husks. To use the kernels for recipes, cut downward using a sharp knife from top to bottom *(left)*.

Cooking

Cook corn on the cob in plenty of boiling salted water until tender. Timing depends on the size of the cobs but 10-15 minutes will normally be enough. Serve them with sea salt and butter, but if the cobs are really sweet, leave out the butter. Stir-fry baby corn cobs briefly and serve in oriental dishes.

Far left: Corn cobs.
Below: Baby corn cobs.

OKRA

History

Okra originated in Africa. In the sixteenth century, when African people were enslaved by the Spanish and shipped to the New World, they took with them the few things they could, including the plants and seeds from home – dried peas, yams, ackee – and okra. This lantern-shaped pod containing rows of seeds oozes a sticky mucilaginous liquid when cooked, and it was popular not only for its subtle flavor but also for thickening soups and stews.

The plant thrived in the tropical climate and by the early nineteenth century, when the slave trade was finally abolished, okra was an important part of the cuisine of the Caribbean and the southern United States. In and around New Orleans, the Creoles, the American-born descendants of European-born settlers, adopted a popular Native American dish called *gumbo*. An essential quality of this famous dish was its thick gluey consistency. The Native Americans used filé powder (the dry pounded leaves of the sassafras tree), but okra was welcomed as a more satisfactory alternative.

Gumbos are now the hallmark of Creole cooking, and in some parts of America, the word "gumbo" is an alternative word for okra itself.

Buying and Storing

Choose young, small pods as older ones are likely to be fibrous. They should be bright green, firm and slightly springy when squeezed. Avoid any that are shriveled or bruised. They will keep for a few days in the salad drawer of the fridge.

Preparing

When cooking whole, trim the top but don't expose the seeds inside or the viscous liquid will ooze into the rest of the dish. If, however, this is what you want, slice thickly or thinly according to the recipe *(right)*. If you want to eliminate some of this liquid, first soak the whole pods in acidulated water (water to which lemon juice has been added) for about an hour.

Cooking

The pods can be steamed, boiled or lightly fried, and then added to or used

with other ingredients. If cooked whole, okra is not mucilaginous but is pleasantly tender. Whether cooked whole or sliced, use garlic, ginger or chili to perk up the flavor, or cook Native American-style, with onions, tomatoes and spices.

Above: Okra.

DRIED BEANS ᴬᴺᴰ PEAS

Dried beans feature in traditional cuisines all over the world, from Mexican refried beans to Italy's *pasta e fagioli*. They are nutritious, providing a good source of protein when combined with rice, and are a marvelous store cupboard standby.

Black-eyed Peas: Sometimes called black-eyed beans, these small cream-colored beans have a black spot or eye. When cooked, they have a tender, creamy texture and a mildly smoky flavor. Black-eyed beans are widely used in Indian cooking.

Chana Dhal: Chana dhal is very similar to yellow split peas but smaller in size and with a slightly sweeter taste. It is used in a variety of vegetable dishes.

Chick-peas: These round beige-colored pulses have a strong, nutty flavor when cooked. As well as being used for curries, chick-peas are also ground into a flour which is widely used in many Indian dishes such as *pakoras* and *bhajees*.

Flageolet Beans: Small oval beans which are either white or pale green in color. They have a very mild, refreshing flavor and feature in classic French dishes.

Green Lentils: Also known as continental lentils, these have quite a strong flavor and retain their shape during cooking. They are very versatile and are used in a number of dishes.

Haricot Beans: Small, white oval beans which come in different varieties. Haricot beans are ideal for Indian cooking because not only do they retain their shape but they also absorb the flavors of the spices.

Kidney Beans: Kidney beans are one of the most popular pulses. They are dark red/brown, kidney-shaped beans with a strong flavor.

Mung Beans: These are small, round green beans with a slightly sweet flavor and creamy texture. When sprouted they produce the familiar bean sprouts.

Red Split Lentils: A readily available lentil that can be used for making dhal. Use instead of toovar dhal.

Toovar Dhal: A dull orange-colored split pea with a very distinctive earthy flavor. Toovar dhal is available plain and in an oily variety.

Soaking and Cooking Tips

Most dried pulses, except lentils, need to be soaked overnight before cooking. Wash the beans thoroughly and remove any small stones and damaged beans. Put into a large bowl and cover with plenty of cold water. When cooking, allow double the volume of water to beans and boil for 10 minutes. This initial boiling period is essential to remove any harmful toxins. Drain, rinse and cook in fresh water. The cooking time for all pulses varies depending on the type and their freshness. Pulses can be cooked in a pressure cooker to save time. Lentils, on the whole, do not need soaking. They should be washed in several changes of cold water before being cooked.

Left: Clockwise from bottom right: Mung beans, Flageolet beans, Chick-peas, Haricot beans, Black-eyed peas, Kidney beans.

Above: Clockwise from top: Red split lentils, Green lentils, Toovar dhal, Chana dhal.

— *SIX* —

SQUASHES

ZUCCHINI

Zucchini are the best loved of all the squashes as they are so versatile. They are quick and easy to cook and are succulent and tender with a delicate, unassuming flavor. Unlike other squashes, they are available all year through.

Vegetables taste best when eaten immediately after they have been picked, and this particularly applies to zucchini. They have a long season and are good to grow since the more you cut, the more the plants produce. Left unchecked, they turn into marrows.

Varieties

The zucchini is classified as a summer squash, *cucurbita pepo*, along with marrows and pattypan squashes.

Zucchini: Sometimes called courgettes, zucchini are basically immature marrows. The word is a diminutive of the Italian *zucca*, meaning gourd, and similarly courgette means miniature *courge*, French for marrow. Zucchini have a deep green skin, with firm pale flesh. The seeds and pith found in marrows have yet to form but are visible in more mature zucchini. Conversely, the prized baby zucchini have no suggestion of seeds or pith and the flesh is completely firm.

Yellow Zucchini: These are bright yellow and somewhat straighter than green zucchini. They have a slightly firmer flesh than green zucchini but are otherwise similar.

Pattypan Squashes: These little squashes look like tiny custard squashes. They can be pale green, yellow or white and have a slightly firmer texture than zucchini, but a similar flavor. They can be sliced and broiled in the same way as zucchini but, to make the most of their size and shape, steam them whole until tender.

Summer Crooknecks: Pale yellow with curves at the neck and a bumpy skin, crooknecks are prepared and cooked in the same way as zucchini.

Italian Zucchini: These very long, thin zucchini are grown in Italy. They are treated liked ordinary zucchini but are strictly a bottle gourd.

Buying and Storing

Zucchini should be firm with a glossy, healthy looking skin. Avoid any that feel soft or generally look limp, as they will be dry and not worth using. Choose small zucchini whenever possible and buy in small quantities as needed.

Preparing

The tiny young zucchini need no preparation at all, and if they still have their flowers, so much the better. Other zucchini should be topped and tailed and then prepared according to the recipe, either sliced or slit for stuffing.

Cooking

Baby zucchini need little or no cooking. Steam them whole or just blanch them. Sliced larger zucchini can be steamed or boiled but take care that they do not overcook as they go soggy very quickly. Alternately, grill, roast or fry them. Try dipping slices in a light batter and then shallow frying in a blend of olive and sunflower oil. To roast, place them in a ovenproof dish, scatter with crushed garlic and a few torn basil leaves and sprinkle with olive oil; then bake in a very hot oven until tender, turning the slices occasionally.

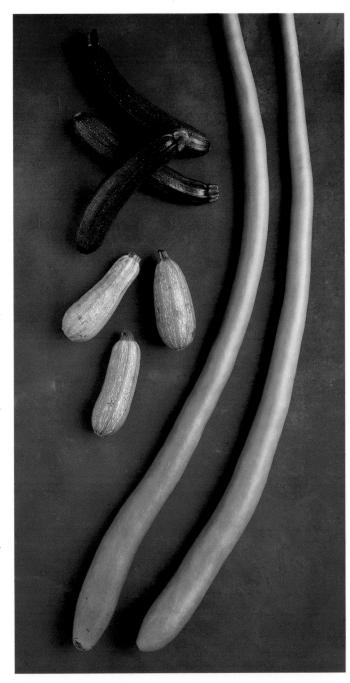

Top left: Pattypan squashes.
Far left: Baby zucchini.
Left: Yellow zucchini.
Right: Italian zucchini beside white and green zucchini.

MARROWS <u>AND</u> SUMMER SQUASHES

Vegetable marrow is classified as a summer squash yet it is rather the poor relation of squashes. Most of the edible flesh is water and at best it is a rather bland vegetable, with a slightly sweet flavor. At worst, it is insipid and if cooked to a mush (which isn't unheard of), it is completely tasteless.

Marrows can be stuffed, although it involves a lot of energy expended for very little reward; but marrow cooked over low heat in butter with no added water (so that it steams in its own juice) brings out the best in it.

History

Marrows, like all the summer and winter squashes, are native to America. Squashes were eaten by Native Americans, traditionally with corn and beans, and in an Iroquois myth the three

vegetables are represented as three inseparable sisters. Although the early explorers would almost certainly have come into contact with them, they were not brought back home, and vegetable marrow was not known in England until the nineteenth century. Once introduced, however, it quickly became very popular. Mrs Beeton gives eight recipes for vegetable marrow and observes that "it is now extensively used." No mention at all is made of zucchini, which of course are simply immature marrows, as any gardener will know.

Varieties

The word "marrow" as a general term tends to refer to the summer squashes. At the end of summer and in the early fall a good variety of the large summer squashes is available.

Vegetable Marrows: This is the proper name for the large prize marrows, beloved of harvest festivals and country fairs. Buy small specimens whenever possible.

Spaghetti Squashes/Marrows: Long and pale yellow, like all marrows these squashes can grow to enormous sizes, but buy small specimens for convenience as well as flavor. They earned their name from the resemblance of the cooked flesh to spaghetti.

To boil a spaghetti squash, first pierce the end, so that the heat can reach the middle, then cook for about 25 minutes or until the skin feels tender. Cut the squash in half lengthwise, remove the seeds, and then fork the strands of flesh out onto a plate. It has a fragrant, almost honey and lemon flavor and tastes good with garlic butter or pesto.

Custard Marrows: These are pretty, pale green squashes with scalloped edges and a similar flavor to zucchini. If possible, buy small specimens, about 4 inches across. Boil these whole until tender, then cut a slice off the tops, scoop out the seeds and serve with a pat of butter.

Buying and Storing

Buy vegetables that have clear, unblemished flesh and avoid any with soft or brown patches. Vegetable marrows and spaghetti squashes will keep for several months provided they are kept in a cool, dark place. Custard marrows will keep up to a week.

Preparing

Wash the skin. For sautéing or steaming, or if the skin is tough, peel it away. For braised marrow, cut into chunks and discard the seeds and pith (*right*). For

stuffing, cut into thick slices or cut lengthwise and discard the seeds and pith.

Cooking

Place chunks of marrow in a heavy-based pan with a little butter, cover and cook until tender. It can then be livened up with garlic, herbs or tomatoes. For stuffed marrow, blanch first, stuff, then cover or wrap it in foil to cook.

Above: Vegetable marrows.
Far left: Spaghetti squashes.
Left: Custard marrows.

PUMPKINS <u>AND</u> WINTER SQUASHES

Pumpkins are the most famous of the winter squashes; aesthetically they are one of nature's most pleasing vegetables for their huge size, their color and the smoothness of their skin. They originated in America and, from a culinary point of view, they have their home here.

The name squash comes from America and as well as pumpkins, the family includes acorn, butternut and turban squashes to name but a few. There are simply hundreds of different squashes, including Sweet Dumpling, Queensland Blue (from Australia), Calabaza, Cushaw and Golden Nugget.

History

The tradition of eating pumpkin at Thanksgiving came from when the Pilgrim Fathers, who had settled in New England and proclaimed a day of thanksgiving and prayer for the harvest. The early tradition was to serve the pumpkin with its head and seeds removed, the cavity filled with milk, honey and spices, and baked until tender. The custom of eating pumpkin at Thanksgiving has remained, but it is now served in a different way: puréed pumpkin, either fresh or canned, is used to make golden tarts.

Varieties

There are a huge number of varieties of winter squashes and, confusingly, many are known by several different names. However, from a cooking point of view, most are interchangeable, although it is best to taste dishes as you cook them, as seasoning may differ from one to the other. In general, they all have a floury and slightly fibrous flesh and a mild, almost bland flavor tinged with sweetness. Because of this blandness, they harmonize well with other ingredients.

Acorn Squashes: These are small and heart-shaped with a beautiful deep green or orange skin, or a mixture of the two. Peel, then use as for pumpkins or bake whole, then split and serve with butter.

Butternut Squashes: Perfectly pear-shaped, these are a buttery color. Use in soups or in any pumpkin recipe.

Delicata Squashes: This pretty pale yellow squash has a succulent yellow

flesh, tasting like a cross between sweet potato and butternut squash.

English Pumpkins: These have a softer flesh than the American variety and are good for soups or, if puréed, combined with potatoes or other root vegetables.

Hubbard Squashes: These large winter squashes have a thick, bumpy, hard shell which can range in color from bright orange to dark green. If they are exceptionally large, they are sometimes sold in halves or large wedges. They have a grainy texture and are best mashed with butter and seasoning.

Kabocha Squashes: Attractive bright green squashes with a pale orange flesh.

They are similar in flavor and texture to acorn squashes and can be prepared and cooked in the same way.

Onion Squashes: Round, yellow or pale orange, onion squashes have a mild flavor, less sweet than pumpkin but still with a slightly fruity or honey taste. They are good in risottos or in most pumpkin recipes, but taste for flavor – you may need to add extra seasoning or sugar.

Above: Clockwise from right: A pumpkin hybrid, Kabocha squash, Acorn squash. Right: Clockwise from top right: Hybrid squash, two Golden Acorn squashes, two small and one large pumpkin.

Buying and Storing

All winter squashes may be stored for long periods. Buy firm, unblemished vegetables with clear smooth skins.

Preparing

For larger squashes, or for those being used for soups or purées, peel and cut into pieces, removing the seeds (*left*).

Cooking

Boil in a little water for about 20 minutes until tender, then mash and serve with butter and plenty of salt and pepper. Smaller squashes can be baked whole in their skins, then halved, seeded and served with butter and maple syrup. Pumpkin and other squashes can also be lightly sautéed in butter before adding stock, cream or chopped tomatoes.

Pumpkins: Large, bright yellow or orange squashes, with a deep orange flesh. They have a sweet, slightly honeyed, flavor and are very much a taste North Americans and Australians grow up with. However, they are not to everyone's liking and some people find them rather cloying. Pumpkin soup, pumpkin bread and pumpkin pie are part of the American tradition, as are faces carved from the shell at Halloween.

EXOTIC GOURDS

While the squashes are native to America, most gourds originated in the Old World – from Africa, India and the Far East. However, over the millennia, seeds crossed water and, over the centuries, people crossed continents so that squashes and gourds are now common all over the world. Both belong to the family *Cucurbitacea,* and both are characterised by their rapid-growing vines.

Bottle Gourds: Bottle gourds are still a familiar sight in Africa, where they are principally grown not for their fruit, but for their dried shells. The gourds can grow to enormous sizes and the shells are used for water bottles, cups and musical instruments. The young fruit can be eaten, but it is extremely bitter and is normally only added to highly flavored stews, like curries.

Chayotes: The chayote (pronounced chow-chow) is a popular gourd in all sorts of regions of the world and can be found in just about any ethnic supermarket, be it Chinese, African, Indian or Caribbean. In each it is known by a different name, christophine being the Caribbean term, but choko, shu-shu and chinchayote among its many other names used elsewhere. Unlike most gourds, it originated in Mexico but was widely grown throughout the tropics after the invasions of the Spanish.

It is a pear-shaped fruit with a large central pit and has a cream-colored or green skin. It has a bland flavor, similar to marrow, and a slightly firmer texture something like pumpkin. It is commonly used in Caribbean cooking, primarily as a side dish or in soufflés. Alternately it can be used raw in salads.

Chinese Bitter Melons: These are a common vegetable in all parts of Asia and go by a myriad of names – bitter gourd and bitter cucumber to name but two. They are popular throughout Asia, eaten when very young, but are extremely bitter and rarely eaten in the West. They are easily recognized as they have warty, spiny skins, looking like a toy dinosaur. The skins are white when young but will probably have ripened to a dark green by the time they appear in the shops.

Most recipes from China suggest halving the gourd, removing the pulp and then slicing before boiling for several minutes to remove their bitterness. They can then be added to stir-fries or other oriental dishes.

Far left: Sweet dumpling.
Left: Pumpkin.
Top right: Chinese bitter melon.
Middle right: Loofah.
Below: Chayote.

Smooth and Angled Loofahs: The smooth loofah must be one of the strangest plants. When young it can be eaten, although it is not much valued. However, the plant is grown almost exclusively for sponges, used everywhere as a back rub in the bath. The ripe loofahs are picked and, once the skin has been stripped off and the seeds shaken out, allowed to dry. The plant then gradually dries to a fibrous skeleton and thence to bathrooms everywhere - so now you know!

Angled or ribbed loofahs are more commonly eaten but again are only edible when young as they become unpleasantly bitter when mature. They taste something like zucchini and are best cooked in a similar way, either fried in butter or cooked with tomatoes, garlic and oil.

CUCUMBERS

The Chinese say food should be enjoyed for its texture as well as flavor; cucumbers have a unique texture and refreshing cool taste. An afternoon tea with cucumber sandwiches, thinly sliced cucumber between wafer thin brown buttered bread, provides a delight of contrasts – the soft bread, the smooth butter and the cool crisp cucumber.

Varieties

English Cucumbers: These are the cucumbers the English are most familiar with. They have fewer seeds and thinner skin than the ridged cucumber.
Gherkins: These are tiny cucumbers with bumpy, almost warty skins and are mostly pickled in vinegar and eaten with cold meats or chopped into mayonnaise.
Kirbys: Small cucumbers, available in the United States and used for pickling.
Ridged Cucumbers: These are smaller than most cucumbers with more seeds and a thick, bumpy skin. The waxed ones need to be peeled before eating but most ridged cucumbers on the European Continent are unwaxed and good without peeling.

Buying and Storing

Cucumbers should be firm from top to bottom. They are often sold prewrapped in plastic and can be stored in the salad drawer of the fridge for up to a week. Remove the plastic packaging once you've "started" a cucumber. Discard once it begins to go soggy.

Preparing

Whether you peel a cucumber or not is a matter of personal preference, but wash it if you don't intend to peel it. Some producers use wax coatings to give a glossy finish and these cucumbers must be peeled. If you are in doubt, buy organic cucumbers. Special citrus peelers can remove strips of peel to give an attractive striped effect when sliced.

Left: Cucumbers.
Above right: Ridged cucumbers.
Above far right: Baby cucumbers.
Below right: Kirbys.

Serving

Thinly sliced cucumber is most frequently served with a light dressing or sour cream. In Greece cucumber is an essential part of a Greek country salad, *horiatiki salata*, cut into thick chunks and served with tomatoes, peppers and feta and dressed simply with olive oil and a little wine vinegar.

Iced cucumber soup is delicious, and cucumber can also be puréed with yogurt, garlic and herbs and served with sour cream stirred in.

Cooking

Cucumbers are normally served raw, but are surprisingly good cooked. Cut the cucumber into wedges, remove the seeds and then simmer for a few minutes until tender. Once drained, return the cucumber to the pan and stir in a little cream and seasoning.

FRUIT

TOMATOES

Next to onions, tomatoes are one of the most important fresh ingredients in the kitchen. In Mediterranean cooking, they are fundamental. Along with garlic and olive oil, they form the basis of so many Italian, Spanish and Provençal recipes that it is hard to find many dishes in which they are not included.

History

Tomatoes are related to potatoes, eggplant and sweet and chili peppers, and all are members of the nightshade family. Some very poisonous members of this family may well have deterred our ancestors from taking to tomatoes. Indeed, the leaves of tomatoes are toxic and can result in a very bad stomach ache.

Tomatoes are native to western South America. By the time of the Spanish invasions in the sixteenth century, they were widely cultivated throughout the whole of South America and Mexico. Hernán Cortés, conqueror of the Aztecs, sent the first tomato plants, a yellow variety, to Spain (no doubt along with the plundered Aztec gold).

However, people did not instinctively take to this "golden apple." English horticulturists mostly grew them as ornamental plants to adorn their gardens and had little positive to say about them as food. Spain is recorded as the first country to use tomatoes in cooking, stewing them with oil and seasoning. Italy followed suit, but elsewhere they were treated with suspicion.

The first red tomatoes arrived in Europe in the eighteenth century, brought to Italy by two Jesuit priests. They were gradually accepted in northern Europe where, by the mid-nineteenth century, they were grown extensively, eaten raw, cooked or used for pickles.

Above right: Red and yellow cherry tomatoes.
Below right: Yellow pear tomatoes.
Opposite above: Round or salad tomatoes on the vine.
Opposite below: Beefsteak tomatoes.

Varieties

There are countless varieties of tomatoes, ranging from the huge beef tomatoes that measure 4 inches across, to tiny cherry tomatoes, not much bigger than a thumb nail. They come in all shapes, too – elongated, plum-shaped or slightly squarish and even pear-shaped.

Beefsteak Tomatoes: Large, ridged and deep red or orange in color, these have a good flavor so are good in salads.

Canned Tomatoes: Keep a store of canned tomatoes, especially in the winter when fresh ones tend to taste insipid. Tomatoes are one of the few vegetables that take well to canning, but steer clear of any that are flavored with garlic or herbs. It is far better to add flavoring yourself.

Cherry Tomatoes: These small, dainty tomatoes were once the prized treasures of gardeners but are now widely available. Although more expensive than round tomatoes, they have a delightful

sweet flavor and are worth paying the extra money for serving in salads or for cooking whole.

Plum Tomatoes: Richly flavored with fewer seeds than regular tomatoes, these Italian-grown tomatoes are usually recommended for cooking, although they can be used in salads.

Round or Salad Tomatoes: These are the common tomatoes found in grocers and supermarkets. They vary in size according to the exact type and season. Sun-ripened tomatoes have the best flavor, however; for through-the-year availability the fruit is often picked and ripened off the plant. These tomatoes are versatile in everyday cooking. Adding a pinch of sugar and taking care to season the dish well helps to overcome any weakness in flavor.

Sun-dried Tomatoes: This is one of the fashionable foods of the late Eighties and early Nineties. They add an evocative flavor to many Mediterranean dishes, but don't use them too indiscriminately.

Tomato Paste: This is good for adding an intense tomato flavor, but use carefully or the flavor will be overpowering. Tubes have screw tops and are better than cans as, once opened, they can be kept for up to 4–6 weeks in the fridge.

Yellow Tomatoes: These are exactly like red tomatoes - they may be round, plum or cherry-sized - except they are yellow.

Buying and Storing

Ideally, tomatoes should be allowed to ripen slowly on the plant so that their flavor can develop. Consequently, home-grown tomatoes are best, followed by those grown and sold locally. When buying from a supermarket or grocer, look at the leafy green tops; the fresher they look the better. Buy locally grown beefsteak or cherry tomatoes for salads and plum tomatoes for rich sauces. Paler tomatoes or those tinged with green will redden if kept in a brown paper bag or the salad drawer of the fridge, but if you intend to use tomatoes right away, buy bright red specimens. Overripe tomatoes, where the skin has split and they seem to be bursting with juice, are excellent in soups. However, check for any sign of mold or decay, as this will spoil all your good efforts.

Preparing

Slice tomatoes across rather than downward for salads and pizza toppings. For wedges, cut downward; halve or quarter and cut into two or three depending on the size of the tomato.

Cooking

Among the many classic tomato dishes is tomato soup, cooked to a delicate orange color with stock or milk, or simmered with vegetables, garlic and basil. Recipes *à la provençale* indicate that tomatoes are in the dish; in Provençal cooking and Italian dishes, tomatoes are used with fish, meat and vegetables, in sauces and stuffings, with pasta and in superb salads. The Italian *tri colore salata* is a combination of large tomatoes, mozzarella and basil (the three colors of the Italian flag). The natural astringency of tomatoes means that, in salads, they need only be sprinkled with a fruity olive oil.

Chopped Tomatoes

Chopped tomatoes add a depth of flavor to all sorts of meat and vegetarian dishes. Ideally, even in fairly rustic meals, the tomatoes should be peeled, since the skin can be irritating to eat once cooked. Some sauces also recommend seeding tomatoes, in which case cut the tomato into halves and scoop out the seeds before chopping (above).

Skinning Tomatoes

Cut a cross in the tops of the tomatoes, then place in a bowl and pour over boiling water. Leave for a minute (*above*), then use a sharp knife to peel away the skin, which should come away easily. Do a few at a time (five at most) otherwise they will begin to cook while soaking; boil water for the next batch when you have finished peeling. The water must be boiling.

EGGPLANTS

Many varieties of eggplants are cultivated and cooked all over the world. In Europe, Asia or America, they feature in a multitude of different dishes.

History

Although eggplant is a member of the nightshade family and thus related to potatoes, tomatoes and peppers, it was not discovered in the New World. The first mention of its cultivation is in China in 5 BC, and it is thought to have been eaten in India long before that. The Moors introduced the eggplant to Spain some 1200 years ago and it was grown in Andalucia. It is likely that they also introduced it to Italy, and possibly from there to other southern and eastern parts of Europe.

In spite of their popularity in Europe, eggplants did not become popular in the United States or Britain until very recently; although previous generations of food writers knew about them, they gave only the occasional recipe for cooking with them.

Above left: Plum tomatoes.
Top: Eggplants.
Above: Baby eggplants.
Left: Japanese eggplants.

Meanwhile, in the southern and eastern parts of Europe, eggplant had become extremely well liked, and today it is one of the most popular vegetables in the Mediterranean. Indeed, Italy, Greece and Turkey claim to have 100 ways of cooking it. In the Middle East, eggplant is also a central part of their cuisine.

Varieties

There are many different varieties of eggplants, differing in color, size and shape according to their country of origin. Small ivory-white and plump eggplants look like large eggs (hence their name in the States; they are called aubergines in the UK). Pretty striped eggplants may be either purple or pink and flecked with white irregular stripes. The Japanese or Asian eggplant is straight and very narrow, ranging in color from a pretty variegated purple and white to a solid purple. It has a tender, slightly sweet flesh. Most eggplants, however, are either glossy purple or almost black and can be long and slim or fat like zeppelins. All eggplants have a similar flavor and texture; they taste bland yet slightly smoky when cooked, and the flesh is spongy to touch when raw, but soft after cooking.

Buying and Storing

Eggplants should feel heavy and firm to the touch, with glossy, unblemished skins. They will keep well in the salad drawer of the fridge for up to two weeks.

Preparing

When frying eggplants for any dish where they need slicing (e.g. ratatouille), it is a good idea to salt the slices first in order to draw out some of their moisture, otherwise, they absorb enormous quantities of oil during cooking (they absorb copious amounts anyway, but

salting reduces this slightly). Salting also used to be advised to reduce their bitterness but today's varieties are rarely bitter.

To salt eggplants, cut into slices, about ¹/₂ inch thick for fried slices, *(top right)* or segments *(above right)* and sprinkle generously with salt. Leave them to drain in a colander for about one hour, then rinse well and gently squeeze out the moisture from each slice or carefully pat dry with a piece of cheesecloth.

Cooking

Eggplant slices can be fried in olive oil, as they are or first coated in batter – both popular Italian and Greek starters.

For moussaka, *parmigiana* and other dishes where eggplant is layered with

other ingredients, fry the slices briefly in olive oil. This gives them a tasty crust, while the inside stays soft.

To make a purée, such as for Poor Man's Caviar, first prick the eggplant all over with a fork and then roast in a moderately hot oven for about 30 minutes until tender. Scoop out the flesh and mix with scallions, lemon juice and olive oil. One of the most famous eggplant dishes is *Imam Bayaldi* – "the Iman fainted" – fried eggplant stuffed with onions, garlic, tomato, spices and lots of olive oil.

Above left: White eggplants.
Below left: Striped eggplants.
Above: Thai eggplants, including white, yellow and Pea eggplants.

PEPPERS

In spite of their name, peppers have nothing to do with the spice pepper used as a seasoning, although early explorers may have been mistaken in thinking the fruit of the shrubby plant looked like the spice they were seeking. It is thanks to this 400-year-old mistake that the name "pepper" has stuck.

History

The journeys Christopher Columbus and the conquistadors made were partly to find the spices Marco Polo had found a hundred years earlier in the Far East. Instead of the Orient, however, Columbus discovered the Americas, and instead of spices, he found maize, potatoes and tomatoes. He would have noted, though, that the Native Americans flavored their food with ground peppers, and since it was hot, like pepper, perhaps wishful thinking colored his objectivity. In any case, he returned with the new vegetables, describing them as peppers and advertising them as more pungent than those from Caucasus.

Varieties

Peppers and chilies are both members of the capsicum family. To distinguish between them, peppers are called sweet peppers, bell peppers and even bullnose peppers and come in a variety of colors – red, green, yellow, white, orange and a dark purple-black.

The color of the pepper tells you something about its flavor. Green peppers are the least mature and have a fresh "raw" flavor. Red peppers are ripened green peppers and are distinctly sweeter. Yellow/orange peppers taste more or less like red peppers, although perhaps slightly less sweet and if you have a fine palate you may be able to detect a difference. Black peppers have a similar flavor to green peppers but when cooked are a bit disappointing as they turn green; so if you buy them for their dramatic color, they are best used in salads.

In Greece and other parts of southern Europe, longer, slimmer peppers are often available which have a more pronounced sweet and pungent flavor than the bell-shaped peppers in the US – although this may be because they are locally picked and therefore absolutely fresh. Whichever is the case, they are quite delicious.

Buying and Storing

Peppers should look glossy and sprightly and feel hard and crisp; avoid any that look wrinkled or have damp soft patches. They will keep for a few days at the bottom of the fridge.

Preparing

To prepare stuffed peppers, cut off the top and then cut away the inner core and pith, and shake out the seeds. The seeds and core are easily removed when halving, quartering or slicing.

Cooking

There are countless ways of cooking peppers. Sliced, they can be fried with onions and garlic in olive oil and then braised with tomatoes and herbs. This is the basic ratatouille; other vegetables, such as zucchini and eggplant, can of course be added.

Peppers can be roasted, either with ratatouille ingredients or with only onions and garlic. Cut into large pieces, place in a roasting pan and sprinkle with olive oil, torn basil and seasoning. Roast in a very hot oven (425°F) for about 30 minutes, turning occasionally. Broiled peppers are another superb dish. Once broiled they can be skinned to reveal a soft, luxurious texture and added to salads.

Above far left: Red, green and orange bell peppers.
Below far left: Yellow bell peppers.
Above left: White bell peppers.
Above right: Purple bell peppers.

Skinning Peppers

Cut the pepper into quarters lengthwise and broil, skin side up (*above*), until the skin is charred and evenly blistered. Place the pieces immediately into a plastic bag (you will need tongs or a fork as they will be hot) and close the top of the bag with a tie or a loose knot. Leave for a few minutes and then remove from the bag and the skin will peel off easily.

CHILIES

Some people apparently become so addicted to the taste of hot food that they carry little jars of chopped dried chilies around with them and scatter them over every meal. Although this is a bit extreme, it is chilies more than any other ingredient that spice up our mealtimes.

Varieties

Chilies are the most important seasoning in the world after salt. Unlike peppers, to which they are closely related, the different varieties of chili can have widely different heat values – from the "just about bearable" to the "knock your head off" variety.

Anaheim Chili: A long, thin chili with a blunt end, named after the Californian city. It can be red or green and has a mild, sweet taste.

Ancho Chili/Pepper: These look like tiny peppers. They are mild enough to taste their underlying sweetness.

Birdseye or Bird Chili: These small red chilies are fiery hot. Also known as pequin chilies.

Cayenne Pepper: This is made from the dried, ground seeds and pods of chilies. The name comes from the capital of French Guiana, north of Brazil, although the cayenne chili does not grow there any longer and the pepper is made from chilies grown all over the world.

Early Jalapeño: A popular American chili, which starts dark green and gradually turns to red.

Habañero: Often called Scotch Bonnet, this is the hottest of all chilies and is small and can be green, red or yellow. Color is no real guide to its heat properties, so don't be fooled into thinking that green ones are mild. They are all *very* hot. The habañero comes from Mexico and is frequently used in Mexican and Caribbean dishes.

Hot Gold Spike: A large, pale, yellow-green fruit grown in the southwestern United States: it is very hot.

Above: Birdseye chilies.
Left: Habañero chilies (in and below bowl) and Yellow wax peppers.

The capsaicin in chilies is most concentrated in the pith inside the pod and this, together with the seeds, should be cut away (*below*) unless you want maximum heat. Capsaicin irritates the skin and especially the eyes, so take care when preparing chilies. Either wear gloves or wash your hands thoroughly after handling chilies. If you rub your eyes, even if you have washed your hands carefully, it will be painful.

Poblano: A small, dark green chili, served whole in Spain either roasted or broiled. They are mostly mild but you can get the rogue fiery one, so beware if eating them whole.

Red Chili: These are long, rather wrinkled chilies which are green at first and then gradually ripen to red. They are of variable hotness and, because they are so long and thin, are rather difficult to prepare.

Serrano Chili: A long, red and extremely hot chili.

Tabasco: A sauce made with chilies, salt and vinegar and first made in New Orleans. It is a fiery sauce, popular in Creole, Caribbean and Mexican cookery – or indeed in any dish requiring last minute heat.

Yellow Wax Pepper: Pale yellow to green, these can vary from mild to hot.

Buying and Storing

Some fresh chilies look wrinkled even in their prime and therefore this is not a good guide to their freshness. They should, however, be unblemished, and avoid any which are soft or bruised.

The substance which makes the chili hot is a volatile oil called capsaicin. This differs not only from one type to another but also from plant to plant, depending on growing conditions; the more the plant has to struggle to survive in terms of light, water, soil, etc, the more capsaicin will be produced. It is therefore impossible to tell how hot a chili will be before tasting, although some types are naturally hotter than others. The belief that green chilies are milder than red ones does not necessarily follow; generally red chilies will have ripened for longer in the sun with the result that they will only be sweeter for all that sunshine. Chilies can be stored in a plastic bag in the fridge for a few days.

Cooking

In Mexican cooking chilies play a vital, and almost central role. It is difficult to think of any savory Mexican dish that does not contain either fresh chilies or some form of processed chili, whether canned, dried or ground. Other cuisines, however, are equally enthusiastic about chilies. They are essential in curries and similar dishes from India and the Far East, and in Caribbean and Creole food they are also used extensively.

If you have developed a tolerance for really hot food, then there is no reason why you shouldn't add as many as you wish. In general, however, use chilies discreetly, if for no better reason than you can't take the heat away if you make a mistake.

Above: Ancho chilies (left) and Anaheim chilies (on board).

PLANTAINS AND GREEN BANANAS

While bananas are well and truly fruit, eaten almost exclusively as a dessert or by themselves as fruit, plantains can reasonably be considered among the vegetable fraternity as they have a definite savory flavor, are normally eaten as a first or main course and can only be eaten once cooked.

Varieties

Plantains: Also known as cooking bananas, these have a coarser flesh and more savory flavor than sweet bananas. While superficially they look exactly like our own bananas, they are, on closer inspection, altogether larger and heavier looking. They can vary in color from the unripe fruit, which is green, through yellow to a mottled black color, which is when the fruit is completely ripe.

Green Bananas: Only certain types of green bananas are used in African and Caribbean cooking, and the "greenish" bananas you find in most western supermarkets are normally eating bananas, just waiting to ripen. If you need green bananas for a recipe, look out for them in West Indian or African stores.

Preparing

Plantains: These are inedible raw and must be cooked before eating. Unless very ripe, the skin can be tricky to remove. With yellow and green plantains, cut the fruit into short lengths, then slit the skin along the natural ridge of each piece of plantain. Gently ease the skin away from the flesh and pull the skin until it peels off completely (*below*).

Once peeled, plantains can be sliced horizontally or into lengths and then roasted or fried. Like bananas, plantains will discolor if exposed to the air so, if not using immediately, sprinkle with lemon juice or place in a bowl of salted water.

Green Bananas: These should be prepared in a similar way. As with plantains, green bananas should not be eaten raw and are usually boiled, either in their skins or not, according to the recipe.

If making green banana crisps, use a potato peeler to produce the thinnest slices (*left*).

If cooking plantains or green bananas in their skins, slit the skin lengthwise along the sides and place in a saucepan of salted water. Bring to the boil, simmer gently for about 20 minutes until tender and then cool. The peel can then easily be removed before slicing.

Cooking and Serving

Plantains and green bananas both have an excellent flavor. In many African and Caribbean recipes they are roasted or fried and then served simply with salt. However, if boiled, they can be sliced and served in a simple salad with a few sliced onions, or added to something far more elaborate like a gado gado salad, with mango, avocado, lettuce and shrimp.

Plantains also make a delicious soup, where they are often teamed with corn. After frying an onion and a little garlic, add two sliced and peeled plantains, together with tomatoes, if liked. Fry gently for a few minutes and then add vegetable stock to cover and one or two sliced chilies, together with about 6 ounces of corn. Simmer gently together until the plantain is tender.

Above left: Plantains.
Below left: Green bananas.
Below: Canned ackee.

ACKEE

Ackee is a tropical fruit which is used in a variety of savory dishes, mainly of Caribbean origin, where the fruit is very popular. The fruit itself is bright red and, when ripe, bursts open to reveal three large black seeds and a soft, creamy flesh resembling scrambled eggs. It has a slightly lemony flavor and is traditionally served with saltfish to make one of Jamaica's national dishes. Only buy ripe fruit as, when under-ripe, certain parts of the fruit are toxic.

However, unless you are visiting the Caribbean you are probably only likely to find ackee in cans, and indeed most recipes call for canned ackee which is a good substitute for the fresh fruit.

Jamaican cooks also use ackee to add a subtle flavor to a variety of vegetable and bean dishes. The canned ackee needs very little cooking, and should be added to dishes in the last few minutes of cooking. Take care when stirring into a dish as it breaks up very easily.

AVOCADOS

The avocado has been known by many names – butter pear and alligator pear to name but two. It earned the title butter pear clearly because of its consistency, but alligator pear was the original Spanish name. Although you would be forgiven for thinking this was due to its knobbly skin (among some varieties anyway), the name in fact derives from the Spanish which was based on the Aztec word, the basically unpronounceable *ahuacatl.* From this to the easily-said alligator and thence to avocado was but a short step.

History

The avocado is a New World fruit, native to Mexico, but while it would have been "discovered" by the Old World explorers, it didn't become a popular food in Europe until the middle of this century, when modern transport meant that growers in California, who started farming avocados in the middle of the nineteenth century, could market this fruit worldwide. Avocados are now also exported by South Africa and Australia.

Nutrition

The avocado is high in protein and carbohydrate. It is one of the few fruits that contains fat, and it is also rich in potassium, Vitamin C, some B vitamins and Vitamin E. Its rich oils, particularly its Vitamin E content, mean that it is not only useful as food, but for skin and hair care too, something the Aztecs and Incas were aware of a thousand years ago. The cosmetic industry may have been in its infancy, but it still knew a good thing when it saw it.

Because of their valuable protein and vitamin content, avocados are a popular food for babies. They are easily blended, and small children generally enjoy their creamy texture and pleasant flavor.

Varieties

There are four varieties: Hass, the purple-black small knobbly avocado, the Ettinger and Fuerte, which are pear-shaped and have smooth green skin, and the Nabal, which is rounder in shape. The black-colored Hass has golden-yellow flesh, while green avocados have pale green to yellow flesh.

Buying and Storing

The big problem in buying avocados is that they're never ripe when you want them to be. How often do you see shoppers standing by the avocado shelves, feeling around for that rare creature, the perfectly ripe avocado? Most times they all feel as hard as rocks; that or else they're hopelessly soft and squashy and clearly past their best. The proper and sensible thing to do is buy fruit a few days before you need it. An unripe avocado will ripen in between 4-7 days at room temperature. Once it is ripe, it will keep well in the fridge for a few days, but you still need to plan well in advance if you want to be sure of the perfect avocado.

The alternative is to hope for the best and keep feeling around until you find a ripe fruit. A perfect avocado should have a clean, unblemished skin without any brown or black patches. If ripe, it should "give" slightly if squeezed gently in the hand, but not so much that it actually feels soft. Over-ripe avocados are really not worth bothering with, however persuasive and generous the offer from the man on the market. The flesh will be unattractively brown and stringy and the bits of good flesh you do manage to salvage will be soft and pulpy. Good for a dip, but nothing much else.

Preparing

Although they are simple fruits, avocados can be the devil to prepare. Once peeled, you are left with a slippery object which is then almost impossible to remove from the stone.

If you intend to eat the avocados in halves, it's fairly simple to just prise out the pit once halved. If you want to slice the fruit, use this tip. The only thing you need is a very sharp knife. Cut the avocado in half, remove the stone and then, with the skin still on, cut through the flesh and the skin to make slices. It is then relatively simple to strip off the peel.

Remember to sprinkle the slices with lemon juice as the flesh discolors once exposed to the air.

Cooking

Most popular raw, avocados can also be baked, broiled or used in sautéed and sauced dishes.

Serving Ideas

As well as shrimp or vinaigrette, a half avocado can hold a mixture of chopped tomatoes and cucumber, a mild garlic cheese dip or a sour cream potato salad. Slices of avocado are delicious served with sliced tomatoes and mozzarella, sprinkled simply with olive oil, lemon juice and plenty of black pepper. Avocado can be chopped and added to a salad, or puréed for a rich dressing.

In Mexico, where avocados grow in abundance, there are countless avocado recipes. Guacamole is perhaps the best known, but they are also eaten in soups and stews and commonly used to garnish tacos and enchiladas.

BREADFRUIT

Breadfruit is the name for a tropical tree that grows on the islands of the South Pacific ocean. The fruit of the tree is about the size of a small melon with a rough rind and a pale, mealy flesh.

Preparing

The fruit should be peeled and the core removed.

Cooking

Breadfruit can be treated like potatoes: the flesh may be boiled, baked or fried. It is a staple food for the people of the Pacific islands who bake the flesh, or dry and grind it for biscuits, bread and puddings. It has a sweet flavor and soft texture when ripe.

*Left: Clockwise from the right: Fuerte,
Hass and Nabal avocados.
Right: Breadfruit.*

SALAD
VEGETABLES

Lettuce

Arugula

Chicory and Radicchio

Radishes

Watercress

Mustard and Cress

LETTUCE

One aspect of lettuce that sets it apart from any other vegetable is that you can only buy it in one form – fresh.

History

Lettuce has been cultivated for thousands of years. In Egyptian times it was sacred to the god Min, and tubs of lettuce were ceremoniously carried before this fertility god. It was then considered a powerful aphrodisiac, yet for the Greeks and the Romans lettuce was thought to have quite the opposite effect, making one sleepy and generally soporific. Chemists today confirm that lettuce contains a hypnotic similar to opium, and in herbal remedies lettuce is recommended for insomniacs.

Varieties

There are hundreds of different varieties of lettuce. Today, an increasing variety is available in stores so that the salad bowl can contain a wealth of color and texture.

Round Lettuces

Sometimes called head or cabbage lettuces, round lettuces have cabbage-like heads and include:
Butterheads: These are the classic lettuces seen in kitchen gardens. They have a pale heart and floppy, loosely packed leaves. They have a pleasant flavor as long as they are fresh.
Crispheads: Crisp lettuces, such as Iceberg, have an excellent crunchy texture and will keep their vitality long after butterheads have faded and died.
Looseheads: These are non-hearting lettuce with loose leaves and include *lollo rosso* and *lollo biondo*, oakleaf lettuce and Red Salad Bowl. Although they are not particularly remarkable for their flavor, they look superb.

Cos Lettuces

The romaine is the only lettuce that would have been known in antiquity. It is known

Above: Butterhead lettuce.
Right: Lollo rosso lettuce.
Above far right: Romaine lettuce.
Below far right: Lamb's lettuce.
Below extreme right: Bibb lettuce.

by two names: cos, derived from the Greek island where it was found by the Romans; and romaine, the name used by the French after it was introduced to France from Rome. There are two romaine lettuces, both with long, erect heads.

Romaine: Considered the most delicious lettuce, this has a firm texture and a faintly nutty taste. It is the correct lettuce for Caesar Salad, one of the classic salads.

Bibb: In appearance Bibbs look like something between a baby romaine and a tightly furled butterhead. They have firm hearts and are enjoyed for their distinct flavor. Like other lettuce hearts, they cope well with being cooked.

LAMB'S LETTUCE OR CORN SALAD

This popular winter leaf does not actually belong to the lettuce family (it is related to Fuller's teasel), but as it makes a lovely addition to salads, this seems a good place to include it. Called *mâche* in France, it has spoon-shaped leaves and an excellent nutty flavor.

Nutrition

As well as containing vitamins A, C and E, lettuce provides potassium, iron and calcium and traces of other minerals.

Buying and Storing

The best lettuce is that fresh from the garden. The next best thing is to buy lettuce from a farm store or pick-your-own (although if fertilizers and pesticides are used, their flavor will be disappointing compared to the organic product).

Nowadays, lettuce is frequently sold ready shredded and packed with herbs etc, an acceptable and convenient form of buying lettuce. Whether you buy lettuce prepacked or from the shelf, it must be fresh. Soil and bugs can be washed off but those with limp or yellow leaves are of no use. Eat lettuce as soon as possible after purchasing; in the meantime keep it in a cool dark place, such as the salad drawer of the fridge.

Making Salads

Salads can be made using only one lettuce or a mixture of many. There are no rules but, when mixing salads, choose leaves to give contrast in texture and color as well as flavor. Fresh herbs, such as parsley, cilantro and basil also add an interesting dimension.

Tear rather than cut the leaves of loose-leafed lettuce; icebergs and other large lettuces are commonly sliced or shredded. Eat as soon as possible after preparing.

Dressings should be well-flavored with a hint of sharpness, but never too astringent. Make them in a blender, a screw-top jar or in a large bowl so that the ingredients can be thoroughly blended. Always use the best possible oils and vinegars, in roughly the proportion of five oil to one vinegar or lemon juice. Use half good olive oil and half sunflower oil, or for a more fragrant dressing, a combination of walnut oil and sunflower oil. A pinch of salt and pepper is essential, French mustard is optional and the addition of a little sugar will blunt the flavor.

Add the dressing to the salad when you're ready to serve – never before.

ARUGULA

Arugula, also called rocket, has a wonderful peppery flavor and is excellent in a mixed green salad. It has small, bright green dandelion-shaped leaves. The Greeks and Romans commonly ate *arugula* in mixed salads, apparently to help counterbalance the dampening effect lettuce had on the libido – arugula's aphrodisiac properties in antiquity are well cataloged. It used to be sown around the statues of Priapus, the mythological Greek god of fertility and protector of gardens and herbs and son of Aphrodite and Dionysus.

Buying and Storing

Arugula is to be found either among the salads or fresh herbs in supermarkets. Buy fresh green leaves and use soon after purchasing. If necessary, the leaves can be kept immersed in cold water.

Preparing and Serving

Discard any discolored leaves. Add arugula to plain green salads, or grind with garlic, pine nuts and olive oil for a dressing for pasta.

Since it has such a striking flavor, a little arugula goes a long way, making it an excellent leaf for garnishing. It tastes superb contrasted with grilled goat cheese, or one or two leaves can be added to sandwiches, or loosely packed into pitta bread pockets along with tomatoes, avocado, peanuts and bean sprouts.

Above left: Oak Leaf lettuce.
Below left: Frisée.
Below: Arugula.

CHICORY AND RADICCHIO

Chicory, radicchio, endive and escarole are all related to each other and when they are tasted together you can easily detect their family resemblance. Their names are occasionally interchanged: chicory is often referred to as Belgian or French endive, and French and Belgian *chicorée* as the English curly endive and the American frisée.

CHICORY

During the late eighteenth century, chicory was grown in Europe for its root, which was added to coffee. A Belgian, M. Brezier, discovered that the white leaves could be eaten, a fact he kept secret during his lifetime; but after his death chicory became a popular vegetable, first in Belgium and later elsewhere in Europe. Its Flemish name is *witloof*, meaning "white leaf," and its characteristic pale leaf is due to its being grown in darkness; the paler it is, the less bitter its flavor.

Chicory can be eaten raw but is commonly cooked, either baked, stir-fried or poached. To eat raw, separate the leaves and serve with fruit, such as oranges or grapefruit, which counteract chicory's slight bitterness.

RADICCHIO

This is one of many varieties developed from wild chicory. It looks like a small lettuce with deep wine-red leaves and striking cream ribs and owes its splendid foliage to careful shading. If it is grown completely in the dark the leaves are marbled pink, and those that have been exposed to some light can be patched with a green or copper color. Its flavor tends to be bitter but contrasts well with green salads. Radicchio can be stir-fried or poached, although the leaves turn dark green when cooked.

FRISÉE AND ESCAROLE

These are robust salad ingredients in both flavor and texture. The curly-leaved frisée looks like a green frizzy mop and the escarole is broad-leaved, but both have a distinct bitter flavor. Serve mixed with each other and a well-flavored dressing. This dampens down the bitter flavor but gives the salad a pleasant "bite."

Preparing

To prepare chicory, take out the core at the base with a sharp knife (*left*) and discard any wilted or damaged leaves. Rinse thoroughly, then dry the leaves.

Above: Chicory.
Above right: Radicchio.
Below right: Escarole.

Preparing Salad Leaves

Pull the leaves away from the stalk, discarding any wilted or damaged leaves.

Wash the leaves in plenty of cold water, swirling gently to make sure all dirt and any insects are washed away.

Place the washed leaves in a soft dish towel and then gently pat dry.

Place in a dry dish towel in a large plastic bag. Chill in the fridge for about 1 hour.

RADISHES

Radishes have a peppery flavor that can almost be felt in the nostrils as you bite into one. Their pungency depends not only on the varieties but also on the soil in which they are grown. Freshly harvested radishes have the most pronounced flavor and crisp texture.

Varieties

Radishes were loved throughout antiquity and consequently there are many varieties worldwide. Both the small red types and the large white radishes are internationally popular.

Red Radishes: These small red orbs have many pretty names, but are mostly sold simply as radishes. They are available all year round, have a deep pink skin, sometimes paler or white at the roots and a firm white flesh. Their peppery flavor is milder in the spring and they are almost always eaten raw. Finely sliced and sandwiched in bread and butter, they make an interesting *hors d'oeuvre.*

French Breakfast Radishes: These are red and white and slightly more elongated than the red radish. They tend to be milder than the red radishes and are popular in France either eaten on their own or served with other raw vegetables as *crudités.*

Daikon or Mooli Radishes: Sometimes known as the oriental radish, the daikon is a smooth-skinned, long, white radish. Those bought in stores have a mild flavor, less peppery than the red radish – perhaps because they lose their flavor after long storage (daikons straight from the garden are hot and peppery). They can be eaten raw or pickled, or added to stir-fries.

Buying and Storing

Buy red radishes that are firm with crisp leaves. If at all possible, buy daikons or moolis which still have their leaves; this is a good indication of their freshness as they wilt quickly. The leaves should be green and lively and the skins clear with no bruises or blemishes. They can be stored in the fridge for a few days.

Preparing and Serving

Red radishes need only to be washed. They can then be sliced or eaten whole by themselves or in salads. You can make a feature of them by slicing into a salad of, say, oranges and walnuts, perhaps with a scattering of arugula and dressed with a walnut oil vinaigrette. To use daikon in a stir-fry, cut into slices and add to the dish for the last few minutes of cooking. It adds not only flavor but also a wonderfully juicy and crunchy texture.

Left: Red radishes.
Above: French breakfast radishes.
Right: Daikon, or Mooli, radishes.

WATERCRESS

Watercress is perhaps the most robustly flavored of all the salad ingredients and a handful of watercress is all you need to perk up a rather dull green salad. It has a distinctive "raw" flavor, both peppery and slightly pungent and this, together with its bright green leaves, make it a popular garnish.

Watercress, as the name suggests, grows in water. It needs fast flowing clean water to thrive and is really only successful around freshwater springs on chalk hills. The first watercress beds were cultivated in Europe, but watercress is now grown worldwide.

WINTER CRESS

Winter cress or land cress is often grown as an alternative to watercress, when flowing water is not available. It looks like a robust form of watercress and indeed has a similar if even more assertive flavor, with a distinct peppery taste. Use as you would use watercress, either in salads or in soups.

Nutrition

Watercress is extremely rich in vitamins A, B2, C, D and E. It is also rich in calcium, potassium and iron and provides significant quantities of sulphur and chloride.

Buying and Storing

Only buy fresh-looking watercress – the darker and larger the leaves the better. Avoid any with wilted or yellow leaves. It will keep for several days in the fridge or better still, submerged in a bowl, or arranged in a jar of cold water, and kept in a cool place.

Preparing and Cooking

Discard any yellow leaves and remove thick stalks which will be too coarse for salads or soups. Small sprigs can be added to salads.

For soups and purées, either blend watercress raw or cook briefly in stock, milk or water. Cooking inevitably destroys some of the nutrients but cooked watercress has a less harsh flavor, while still retaining its characteristic peppery taste.

MUSTARD <u>AND</u> CRESS

Mustard and cress are often grown together, to provide spicy greenery as a garnish or for salads. They are available all year through.

Mustard seedlings germinate 3-4 days sooner than the cress, so if you buy mustard and cress from the supermarket, or grow your own on the windowsill, initially the punnets will only show mustard seedlings.

History

Cress has been grown for thousands of years, known first to the Persians. There is a story that the Persians would always eat cress before they baked bread, and there are other references in antiquity to people eating cress with bread.

Serving

Today mustard and cress are often enjoyed in sandwiches, either served simply on buttered bread, or with avocado or cucumber added. Cress probably wouldn't be substantial enough as a salad in itself, but, with its faint spicy flavor, it can perk up a plain green salad, and it is also excellent in a tomato salad, dressed simply with olive oil and tarragon vinegar.

Above left: Watercress.
Below left: Winter cress.
Above right: Mustard seedlings.
Right: Cress seedlings.

NINE

MUSHROOMS

White Mushrooms

Field Mushrooms

Woodland Mushrooms

*Wild Mushrooms
and Other Fungi*

WHITE MUSHROOMS

wrapped cartons, transfer loose to the bottom of the fridge as soon as possible. They will keep only for a day or two.

Preparing

Mushrooms should not be washed but wiped with a damp cloth or a piece of paper towel (*below*). This is partly because you don't want to increase their water content, and also because they should be fried as dry as possible.

Unless the skins are very discolored, it should not be necessary to peel them, although you probably will need to trim the very base of the stem.

Mushrooms are generally cooked, although some white mushrooms are served raw in salads. Eat them quickly; after frying they can go soft and flabby.

History

In the past, mushrooms have had a firm association with the supernatural and even today their connection with the mysterious side of life hasn't completely disappeared. Fairy rings – circles of mushrooms – inexplicably appear overnight in woods and fields and thunder is still thought to bring forth fresh crops of mushrooms.

Many types of mushrooms and fungi are either poisonous or hallucinogenic, and in the past their poisons have been distilled for various murderous reasons.

The use of the term mushroom to mean edible species, and toadstool to mean those considered poisonous, has no scientific basis, and there is no simple rule for distinguishing between the two. Picking wild mushrooms is not safe unless you are confident about identifying edible types. In France during the autumn, people take the wild mushrooms they have gathered to the local pharmacy, where safe mushrooms are identified.

Varieties

White/Button Mushrooms: Cultivated mushrooms are widely available in stores and are sold when very young and tiny. The slightly larger ones are known as closed cap, while larger ones still are open capped, or open cup, mushrooms. They have ivory or white caps with pinky/beige gills that darken as they mature. All have a pleasant flavor.

Cremini Mushrooms: These have a thicker stem and a darker, pale brown cap. They have a more pronounced "mushroomy" flavor and a meatier texture than white mushrooms.

Buying and Storing

It is easy to see whether or not white mushrooms are fresh – their caps will be clean and white, without bruises or blemishes. The longer they stay on the shelves, the darker and more discolored the caps become, while the gills underneath turn from pink to brown.

If possible, use the paper bags provided in many supermarkets nowadays when buying mushrooms. Mushrooms in plastic bags sweat in their own heat, eventually turning slippery and unappetizing. If you have no choice or you buy mushrooms in cellophane-

Cooking

Mushrooms are largely composed of water and shrink noticeably during cooking. They also take up a lot of fat as they cook so it is best to use butter or a good olive oil for frying. Fry mushrooms briskly over a moderately high heat so that as they shrink the water evaporates and they don't stew in their own juice. For the same reason do not fry too many mushrooms at once in the same pan.

Above: White mushrooms.
Top right: Flat mushrooms.
Far right: Field mushrooms.
Right: Cremini mushrooms (top) and open capped or cup mushrooms.

FIELD MUSHROOMS

Field mushrooms are the wild relatives of the cultivated mushroom and when cooked have a wonderful aroma. Flat mushrooms, although indistinguishable from field mushrooms in appearance, have probably been cultivated and are also excellent. Connoisseurs say that only wild mushrooms have any flavor but many would argue against this. However, if you know where to find field mushrooms, keep the secret to yourself (most mushroom devotees seem to know this) and count yourself lucky!

Buying and Storing

Field mushrooms are sometimes available during the autumn in farm stores. Since they are likely to have been picked recently, they should be fresh unless obviously wilting. Unless you intend to stuff them, don't worry if they are broken in places as you will be slicing them anyway. Use as soon as possible after purchase.

Preparing

Trim the stalk bottoms if necessary and wipe the caps with a damp cloth. Slice according to the recipe.

Cooking

For true field mushrooms, you need do nothing more complicated than simply fry them in butter or olive oil with a suggestion of garlic if liked. However, like flat mushrooms, field mushrooms can be used for stuffing, in soups or indeed any mushroom recipe. They are darker than white mushrooms and will color soups and sauces brown, but the flavor will be extremely good.

When stuffing mushrooms, gently fry the caps on both sides for a few minutes. The stalks can be chopped and added to the stuffing or can be used for soups or stocks.

WOODLAND MUSHROOMS

Varieties

Ceps: Popular in France, where they are known as *cèpes* and in Italy where they are called *porcini*, these meaty, bun-shaped mushrooms have a fine almost suede-like texture and a good flavor. Instead of gills they have a spongy texture beneath the cap and unless they are very young it is best to scrape this away as it goes soggy when cooked. Ceps are excellent fried in oil or butter over a brisk heat to evaporate the liquid and then added to omelets.

Alternately, an Italian way of cooking is to remove the stalk and the spongy tubes, and brush the tops with olive oil. Broil for about 10 minutes under a moderate broiler and then turn them over and pour olive oil and a sprinkling of garlic into the center. Broil for a further 5 minutes and then serve sprinkled with seasoning and parsley.

Chanterelles: Frilly, trumpet-shaped chanterelles are delicate mushrooms which range in color from cream to a vivid yellow. Later, winter chanterelles have grayish-lilac gills on the underside of their dark caps. Chanterelles have a delicate, slightly fruity flavor and a firm, almost rubbery texture. They are difficult to clean as their tiny gills tend to trap grit and earth. Rinse them gently under cold running water and then shake dry. Fry in butter over a gentle heat to start with so they exude their liquid and then increase the heat to boil it off. They are delicious with scrambled eggs, or served by themselves with finely cut toast.

Horn of Plenty/Black Trumpets: Taking its name from its shape, this mushroom ranges in color from mid-brown to black. As it is hollow, it will need to be brushed well to clean or, if a large specimen, sliced in half. It is very versatile, but goes particularly well with fish.

Morels: These are the first mushroom of the year, appearing not in autumn but in spring. In Scandinavia they are called the "truffles of the north" and are considered among the great edible fungi. They are cone-shaped with a crinkled spongy cap but are hollow inside. You will need to wash them well under running water as insects tend to creep into their dark crevices. Morels need longer cooking than most mushrooms: sauté them in butter, add a squeeze of lemon and then cover and simmer for up to an hour until tender. The juices can then be thickened with cream or egg yolks.

Dried Mushrooms: Most wild mushrooms are available dried. To reconstitute, soak in warm water for about 20-30 minutes; in the case of morels when they are added to stews, soak for about 10 minutes. Dried wild mushrooms, particularly ceps, have an intense flavor.

Left: Clockwise from the top: Ceps, Horn of Plenty, Chanterelles.
Above right: Dried mushrooms.
Above left: Morels.
Right: Winter chanterelles.

WILD MUSHROOMS <u>AND</u> OTHER FUNGI

Mushroom gathering, a seasonal event throughout Eastern Europe, Italy and France, is increasingly popular. The French are particularly enthusiastic: in autumn whole families drive to secret locations to comb the ground for prizes like shaggy ink caps or ceps. Wild mushrooms are sold in supermarkets.

OYSTER MUSHROOMS

These ear-shaped fungi grow on rotting wood. Cap, gills and stem are all the same color, which can be grayish brown, pink or yellow. They are now widely cultivated, although they are generally thought of as wild mushrooms. Delicious both in flavor and texture, they are softer than the white mushroom when cooked but seem more substantial, having more "bite" to them.

Buying and Storing

Fresh specimens are erect and lively looking with clear gills and smooth caps. They are often sold packed in plastic boxes under cellophane wrappings and

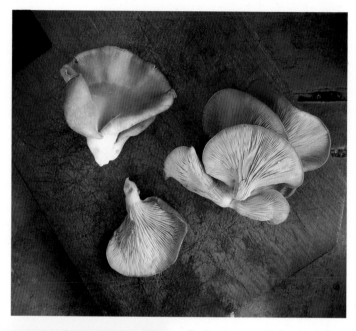

will wilt and go soggy if left on the shelf for too long. Once purchased, remove them from the plastic packaging and use as soon as possible.

Preparing

Oyster mushrooms rarely need trimming at all but if they are large, tear rather than cut them into pieces. In very large specimens the stems can be tough and should be discarded.

Cooking

Fry in butter until tender – they take less time to cook than white mushrooms. Do not overcook oyster mushrooms as the flavor will be lost and the soft texture will become more rubbery.

Left: Pink and yellow oyster mushrooms.
Above: Gray oyster mushrooms.

ENOKITAKI MUSHROOMS

This is another Japanese mushroom. The wild variety is orangy-brown with shiny caps but outside Japan, you will probably only be able to find the cultivated variety, which are similarly fine, with pin-size heads, but are pale colored with snowy white caps. They have a fine, sweet and almost fruity flavor. In Japanese cookery they are added to salads or used as a garnish for soups or hot dishes. Since they become tough if overcooked, add enokitaki mushrooms at the very last minute of cooking.

SHIITAKE MUSHROOMS

These Japanese fungi are now commonly available in supermarkets. They are among a variety of tree mushrooms (called *take* in Japan, the *shii* being the hardwood tree from which they are harvested). They have a meaty, slightly acid flavor and a distinct slippery texture. Shiitake mushrooms, though once only available in oriental stores, are now widely available in most supermarkets. Unlike white mushrooms that can be flash-fried, shiitake need to be cooked through, although even this only takes 3–5 minutes. Add them to stir-fries for a delicious flavor and texture. Alterna-tively, fry them in oil until tender. Sprinkle with sesame oil and then serve with a little soy sauce.

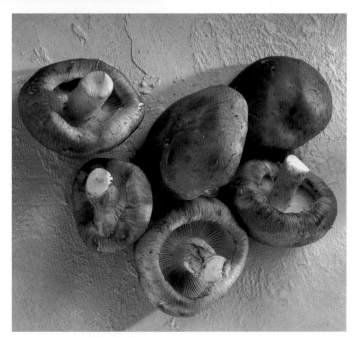

Above: Enokitaki mushrooms.
Right: Shiitake mushrooms.

INDEX

NOTES

NOTES

Notes

NOTES